BBC goodfood

BEST BREADS

Editor **Esther Clark**

T0159848

BOOKS

BBC Books, an imprint of Ebury Publishing
20 Vauxhall Bridge Road,
London SW1V 2SA

BBC Books is part of the Penguin Random House group of companies whose addresses can be found at
global.penguinrandomhouse.com

Penguin
Random House
UK

First published by BBC Books in 2022

www.penguin.co.uk

A CIP catalogue record for this book is available from the British Library

ISBN 9781785947872

Printed and bound in Latvia by Livonia Print

Project Editors: Nell Warner and Kay Halsey
Design: Interstate Creative Partners Ltd and Peppis Designworks
Cover Design: Two Associates
Production: Catherine Ngwong
Picture Researcher: Gabby Harrington

MIX
Paper from
responsible sources
FSC® C018179

PICTURE AND RECIPE CREDITS

BBC Books would like to thank the following people for providing photos. While every effort has been made to trace and
acknowledge all photographers, we should like to apologise should there be any errors or omissions.

Vinny Whiteman p7, Sam Stowell p7, p18, p48, P124, p110, p140, p200; Rob Streeter p20, p72; Will Heap p22, p60, p86, p96, p132,
p138, p142, p152, p188; Nassima Rothacker p26; David Munns p32, p182, p186; Emma Boyns p94; Clare Winfield p76, p162; Tom
Regester p34, p104, p106, p156, p166, p168, p190; Will Heap p70, p196; Toby Scott p98, p146, p148; Myles New p7, p14, p16, p28,
p36, p40, p42, p46, p50, p52, p54, p56, p68, p88, p90, p112, p116, p130, p144, p150, p164, p204, p206, p210; David Cotsworth p30;
Mike English p62, p64, p74, p92, p134, p172, p174, p178, p192, p198, p208; Peter Cassidy p120; Jonathan Gregson p118, p128,
p194; Helen Cathcart p78; Stuart Ovenden p80; Philip Webb p84, p184; Karen Thomas p158, p202; Cameron Watt; James Lee
p108; Alex Luck p114; Melissa Reynolds-James p102; Edd Kimber p126; Yuki Sugiura p170;

All the recipes in this book were created by the editorial team at *Good Food* and by regular contributors to BBC Magazines.

Contents

....

Introduction

· ·

This easy-to-use bread book takes you through a range of methods, from basic breads to sourdough and sweetened, enriched bakes. It is perfect for those who are new to baking as well as those who are already well-seasoned bakers, ready to try out some new recipes and ideas. It's time to get lost in a world of flour and yeast with this fantastic bread companion, packed full of foolproof tried-and-tested recipes from the renowned *BBC Good Food* team.

FLOUR

Most breads use a 'strong' bread flour, whether they are white or brown, which is the most common flour to use in yeasted breads. Strong flour has about 12.5 per cent protein, which is far higher than a plain flour, and this makes the bread much better structurally. It also helps suspend and hold the air bubbles created in bread dough. Using strong bread flour is what gives bread its chewy and springy texture. If you want to mix things up, you can substitute a percentage of bread flour for another flour. For instance, you could use 15 per cent rye flour or spelt flour. This quantity shouldn't affect the overall texture too much and will give your bread a more complex flavour.

YEAST

Most of these recipes use a dried yeast or a dried fast-action yeast. These yeasts can be purchased in the baking section of the supermarket. Dried yeast will need to be awoken and 'activated' in a little warm water before using, whereas fast-action yeast can simply be combined into the dried ingredients and used straight away.

Both these yeasts help to leaven bread and give it its light and airy texture.

Store dried yeasts in a cool, dark place and do not use post their sell-by-date. Yeast loses its activation properties over time.

Fresh yeast can be substituted for dried yeast. Use double the quantity of fresh yeast as that specified for dried yeast in a recipe (so if a recipe specifies a 7g sachet of dried fast-action yeast, use 14g fresh). Dissolve the yeast in just warm water, no hotter than blood temperature, and leave to activate for 10 mins before using. Store fresh yeast in your fridge and keep it for no longer than 2 weeks.

WATER

The water used in breads is incredibly important. It should be neither too cold nor too hot. Water that's too cold won't activate the yeast in the dough and will stop the bread from rising. Water that's too hot will kill the yeast and you will end up again with no rise. Make sure you test your water temperature before using. It should be lukewarm – warm enough to dip a finger into – somewhere between 41–46C (105–115F), which can be tested using a probe thermometer for accuracy. In time and through experience, it will become easier to gauge the right temperature for your water just by touch.

SALT

Salt is key in a yeasted dough. Never be tempted to leave it out. Firstly, that would affect the flavour tremendously. Without salt, the bread will have a yeasty, underbaked and bland flavour. Secondly, it will not rise. Salt strengthens the gluten in your dough, helping with structure and final texture.

CLASSIC KNEADING (PICS 1 & 2)

Bread is kneaded to develop the gluten and turn a rough dough into a smooth, elastic one. Bread can be kneaded by hand or in a stand mixer. If you do have a stand mixer, this will save you time. To knead

bread by hand, try not to dust the surface with too much flour; bread dough is sticky, but it will become less so as you work it. Adding too much flour when you knead can result in a stiffer dough. If you have a wooden non-stick or stainless steel surface, you can oil it instead and lift and fold the dough on it instead of kneading, which will have the same effect. You have to handle the dough lightly with your fingertips when you do this.

Sourdough is kneaded in a different manner, with most of the work done by leaving the bread ingredients to change on their own (all bread dough will do this eventually, but the higher water content of sourdough makes the process more efficient and gives a better result). The kneading process is then more of a stretching process, designed to trap air in the bread dough. This takes less time than kneading a yeasted bread dough.

SOURDOUGH KNEADING (PICS 3 & 4)
Follow this method each time you make sourdough bread. As you make more and more bread, your technique will improve.

1 Wet your hands, grab the dough from one side and stretch it over itself, then repeat with the other side. The dough should stretch without much effort. Keep your hands wet so the dough doesn't stick. This stretching technique helps develop the gluten.

2 Pick the dough up and curl it around onto itself, folding the top

over the bottom, then cover and leave for another 20–30 mins. Repeat this process 2 more times (3 in total) – the bread will get more and more smooth and elastic – then leave the dough for another 2–3 hrs until it's risen by about 30 per cent and looks bubbly and soft.

INITIAL SHAPING FOR SOURDOUGH

This stage is what gives your loaf structure. The more work you put into the structure of your loaf, the better the crumb will be when you bake it.

1 Using a rubber spatula, scrape the dough out onto a lightly floured work surface. If you are making 2 loaves, split the dough. Fold each piece onto itself to create a ball. Do this by stretching the sides downwards and tucking them under the ball. Hold the ball in both hands as you do so, moving it quickly so it doesn't stick. Put on the work surface and leave, uncovered, for 30 mins. The dough will spread out during this time.

2 Scrape up a ball of dough and fold it onto itself to create a tight ball that's trapped in all the air. Fold the sides down and pinch them at the base to do this. The more air you incorporate, the lighter your loaf will be.

SCORING LOAVES

The bread needs to spring open somewhere, and you need to control where this happens or it could burst open anywhere. If you only ever want to make a couple of slashes in a loaf, there is no need to buy a lame (a baker's knife), but if you want to make fancier patterns, you will need one. They're easy to find in kitchenware shops or online. If you are planning on making a pattern, then you will need to balance it with a big score somewhere, often down one side, to let the bread expand. Where you want the bread to open, it's best to hold the lame at a 45-degree angle, which will give you a trademark 'ear' shape. Where you want the scores to open just a little, slash the bread straight down. To highlight your scoring, first dust the loaf with flour – the easiest way to do this is using a small sieve.

BAKING SOURDOUGH USING THE CASEROLE METHOD

Once the oven is turned on, put a lidded casserole dish in the oven to heat. Cut a sheet of baking parchment into a square slightly larger than the base of one of the loaves. Carefully remove the hot casserole dish from the oven and remove the lid. Invert one loaf (from the proving basket) onto the baking parchment, then, working quickly, score the top at an angle using a baker's lame or very sharp knife (see opposite). Use the corners of the parchment to lift the loaf into the casserole dish. Cover with the lid. and bake for 30 mins, then carefully uncover and continue to bake for another 10 mins (or longer for a darker finish). Carefully lift the bread out of the dish using a spatula, transfer to a wire rack and leave to cool to room temperature before slicing. Repeat with the second loaf.

Notes & conversion tables

NOTES ON THE RECIPES
- Eggs are large in the UK and Australia and extra large in America unless stated.
- Plain and self-raising flour is white unless otherwise stated.
- Wash fresh produce before preparation.
- Recipes contain nutritional analyses for 'sugars', which means the total sugar content, including all natural sugars in the ingredients, unless otherwise stated.

OVEN TEMPERATURES

GAS	°C	°C FAN	°F	OVEN TEMP.
¼	110	90	225	Very cool
½	120	100	250	Very cool
1	140	120	275	Cool or slow
2	150	130	300	Cool or slow
3	160	140	325	Warm
4	180	160	350	Moderate
5	190	170	375	Moderately hot
6	200	180	400	Fairly hot
7	220	200	425	Hot
8	230	210	450	Very hot
9	240	220	475	Very hot

APPROXIMATE WEIGHT CONVERSIONS
Cup measurements, which are used in Australia and America, have not been listed here as they vary from ingredient to ingredient. Kitchen scales should be used to measure dry/solid ingredients.

Good Food cares about sustainable sourcing and animal welfare. Where possible, free-range eggs have been used when recipes were originally tested.

SPOON MEASURES

Spoon measurements are level unless otherwise specified.

- 1 teaspoon (tsp) = 5ml
- 1 tablespoon (tbsp) = 15ml
- 1 Australian tablespoon = 20ml (cooks in Australia should measure 3 teaspoons where 1 tablespoon is specified in a recipe)

APPROXIMATE LIQUID CONVERSIONS

METRIC	IMPERIAL	AUS	US
50ml	2fl oz	¼ cup	¼ cup
125ml	4fl oz	½ cup	½ cup
175ml	6fl oz	¾ cup	¾ cup
225ml	8fl oz	1 cup	1 cup
300ml	10fl oz/½ pint	½ pint	1¼ cups
450ml	16fl oz	2 cups	2 cups/1 pint
600ml	20fl oz/1 pint	1 pint	2½ cups
1 litre	35fl oz/1¾ pints	1¾ pints	1 quart

Chapter 1

CLASSIC BREADS

· ·

This chapter has bread making for the novice baker as well as the more advanced. The selection of familiar breads are all made using traditional dried yeast and range from easier to trickier loaves and rolls. Escape to the kitchen and get lost in the art of baking, with everything from a classic white loaf to buttery, enriched brioche and traditional Turkish simit bread.

Easy white bread

This soft white loaf is easy to make and fantastic for sandwiches and toasting. You can use the same method with strong wholemeal flour or do a mix of half and half.

 PREP 20 mins + proving COOK 30 mins   MAKES 1 loaf (cuts into 8–10 slices)

- 500g strong white bread flour, plus extra for dusting
- 2 tsp salt
- 7g sachet fast-action dried yeast
- 3 tbsp olive oil, plus extra for greasing

1 Mix the flour, salt and yeast in a large bowl.
2 Make a well in the centre, then add the oil and 300ml water and mix well. If the dough seems a little stiff, add another 1–2 tbsp water and mix well. Tip onto a lightly floured work surface and knead using your hands or a stand mixer for around 10 mins.
3 Once the dough is satin-smooth, place it in a lightly oiled bowl and cover with cling film. Leave to rise for 1 hour until doubled in size or place in the fridge overnight.
4 Line a baking tray with parchment. Knock back the dough (punch the air out and pull the dough in on itself) then gently mould the dough into a ball. Place on the parchment to prove for a further hour until doubled in size.
5 Heat the oven to 220C/fan 200C/gas 7.
6 Dust the loaf with extra flour and cut a cross 6cm long into the top with a sharp knife.
7 Bake for 25–30 mins until golden brown and the loaf sounds hollow when tapped underneath. Cool on a wire rack.

Nutrition per slice (10)
energy 204 kcals, fat 4g, saturates 1g, carbs 38g, sugars 0g, fibre 2g, protein 6g, salt 1g

Easy bread rolls

Bake these simple white bread rolls for sandwiches, burger buns or to dunk in soup. Using only a handful of ingredients, bread making has never been so easy.

 PREP 30 mins + proving COOK 30 mins MAKES 8

- 500g strong white bread flour, plus extra for dusting
- 7g sachet fast-action dried yeast
- 1 tsp white caster sugar
- 2 tsp fine salt
- 1 tsp sunflower oil, plus extra for greasing

1 Tip the flour, yeast, sugar, salt and oil into a bowl. Pour over 325ml warm water, then mix until it comes together as a shaggy dough. Cover and leave for 10 mins.

2 Lightly oil your work surface and tip the dough onto it. Knead for at least 10 mins until tighter and springy – if you have a stand mixer you can do this with a dough hook for 5 mins. Pull the dough into a ball and put in a clean, oiled bowl. Leave for 1 hr until doubled in size.

3 Tip the dough onto a lightly floured surface, roll into a long sausage and divide into 8 pieces. Roll each into a tight ball and put on a dusted baking tray, leaving room between each ball for rising. Cover with a damp tea towel and leave in a warm place to prove for 40 mins–1 hr or until almost doubled in size.

4 Heat the oven to 230C/210C fan/gas 8. When the dough is ready, dust with a bit more flour. (If you like, glaze with milk or egg and top with seeds.) Bake for 25–30mins, until light brown and hollow sounding when tapped on the base. Leave to cool on a wire rack.

Nutrition per roll
energy 246 kcals, fat 2g, saturates 0g, carbs 48g, sugars 1g, fibre 2g, protein 8g, salt 1.2g

Seeded wholemeal loaf

This hearty, wholesome bread is rich in flavour and packed with seeds – try pumpkin, sunflower, poppy or linseeds.

 PREP 35 mins + proving COOK 45 mins   MAKES 1 loaf (cuts into 10–12 slices)

- 400g strong wholemeal bread flour
- 100g spelt flour
- 7g sachet fast-action dried yeast
- 1 tsp fine salt
- 1 tbsp black treacle
- oil, for greasing
- 50g mixed seeds (we used pumpkin, sunflower, poppy and linseeds)
- 1 egg yolk, loosened with a fork

1 Combine the flours, yeast and salt. Mix the treacle with 250ml warm water. Stir into the flour to make a slightly sticky dough. If you need more water, splash in 1 tbsp at a time.

2 Knead the dough on a lightly floured surface for 10 mins or in a stand mixer for 5–7 mins. Your dough should be smooth and elastic when it's ready. Place in a lightly oiled bowl, flip the dough over to coat it in oil, then cover with a sheet of oiled cling film. Leave in a warm place until doubled in size – this will take about 1 hr. Lightly oil a 900g loaf tin.

3 Once doubled, knead for 3–5 mins to knock out air bubbles. Add most of the seeds and work in. Shape into an oval the same size as the tin, put in and leave, covered with oiled cling film, for 30–45 mins until nearly doubled. Heat the oven to 200C/180C fan/gas 6.

4 When it's ready, glaze with egg and sprinkle over the remaining seeds. Bake for 40–45 mins until golden – if you tip out of the tin and tap the bottom, it should sound hollow. Cool on a wire rack for at least 30 mins before slicing.

Nutrition per slice (12)
energy 180 kcals, fat 3g, saturates 1g, carbs 29g, sugars 2g, fibre 4g, protein 7g, salt 0.43g

Tiger bread

• •

With its iconic crackled crust and pillowy centre, tiger bread is a fantastic baking recipe to have up your sleeve. Our easy recipe makes a great weekend project.

 PREP 25 mins + proving COOK 35 mins   MAKES 1 loaf (cuts into 10–12 slices)

- 500g strong white bread flour, plus extra for kneading
- 7g sachet fast-action dried yeast
- 1½ tsp caster sugar
- 1½ tsp fine sea salt
- 300–350ml warm water
- oil, for greasing

FOR THE TOPPING
- 90g rice flour
- ½ x 7g sachet fast-action dried yeast
- ¼ tsp salt
- 1 tsp golden caster sugar
- ½ tbsp toasted sesame oil
- 90ml warm water

1 Tip the flour into a bowl. Stir through the yeast, sugar and salt. Make a well in the middle and gradually pour in the water. Swiftly mix together, then turn out onto a lightly floured surface. Knead for 8–10 mins until smooth and elastic. Lightly oil a large mixing bowl, then put the dough in the bowl, cover and leave in a warm place for 1 hr or until doubled in size.

2 Once the dough has risen, tip onto a worktop and knead 3 times. Shape into an oval. Lightly flour a baking sheet and sit the loaf on it. Cover loosely with oiled cling film and leave for 45 mins–1 hr until doubled in size again.

3 Heat the oven to 200C/180C fan/gas 6. Whisk together all the topping ingredients until you get a spreadable paste, adding more water and/or flour if necessary, then rest for 5 mins. Gently spread the mixture over the loaf with a palette knife. Place the baking sheet in the centre of the oven and bake for 35 mins. Once cooked, the loaf should sound hollow when the base is tapped and should feel light for its size. Cool completely before slicing.

• •

Nutrition per slice (12)
energy 189 kcals, fat 1g, saturates 0.2g, carbs 38g, sugars 1g, fibre 2g, protein 6g, salt 0.72g

Pitta bread

Rustle up homemade pitta bread to serve with dips or as a side dish to mop up juices. You can easily make them ahead and freeze them for a fail-safe snack.

 PREP 20 mins + proving COOK 40 mins MAKES 8

- 2 tsp fast-action dried yeast
- 500g strong white bread flour, plus extra for dusting
- 2 tsp salt
- 1 tbsp olive oil, plus extra for greasing

1 Mix the yeast with 300ml warm water. Leave to sit for 5 mins until super bubbly, then tip in the flour, salt and oil. Bring together into a soft dough. Don't worry if it looks a little rough.

2 Tip the dough onto a lightly floured work surface. Knead for 5–10 mins until you have a soft, smooth and elastic dough. Try to knead using as little flour as possible – this will keep the pittas light and airy. Place in a lightly oiled bowl, cover with a tea towel and leave to double in size for approximately 1 hour.

3 Heat the oven as high as it will go (ideally 250C/230C fan/gas 9) and put a large baking tray on the middle shelf to get searingly hot. Divide the dough into 8 balls, then flatten each into a disc. On a lightly floured surface, roll into 20cm x 15cm, 3–5mm thick ovals.

4 Remove the hot tray, dust with flour and put the pittas onto it – you may have to do this in batches. Return swiftly to the oven and bake for 4–5 mins, or until puffed up and pale golden. Wrap in a clean tea towel to keep soft while the others cook.

Nutrition per pitta
energy 246 kcals, fat 2g saturates 0.4g carbs 47g sugars 0.3g fibre 2g protein 8g salt 1g

Rye bread

This rye bread recipe is lower in gluten than your average white loaf. This recipe uses white or wholemeal flour to give a light texture but you can experiment with ratios.

 PREP 50 mins + proving COOK 30 mins   MAKES 1 loaf (cuts into 8 slices)

- 200g rye flour, plus extra for dusting
- 200g strong white or wholemeal bread flour
- 7g sachet fast-action dried yeast
- ½ tsp fine salt
- 1 tbsp honey
- oil, for greasing
- 1 tsp caraway seeds (optional)

1 Mix the flours, yeast and salt in a bowl. Mix the honey with 250ml warm water, pour into the bowl and mix to form a dough. If the dough looks too dry, add more warm water until you have a soft dough. Tip out onto your work surface and knead for 10 mins until smooth. Rye contains less gluten than white flour, so the dough will not feel as springy as usual.

2 Put in a well-oiled bowl, cover with cling film and leave in a warm place for 1–2 hrs, or until roughly doubled in size. Flour a 900g loaf tin.

3 Tip the dough back onto your work surface and knead briefly to knock out air bubbles. If using caraway seeds, work these in. Shape into a smooth oval and pop into the tin. Cover with oiled cling film and leave somewhere warm for 1–1½ hrs, or until doubled in size.

4 Heat the oven to 220C/200C fan/gas 7. Remove the cling film and dust with rye flour. Slash a few incisions on an angle then bake for 30 mins until dark brown and hollow sounding when tapped. Transfer to a wire rack and leave to cool for at least 20 mins.

Nutrition per slice
energy 170 kcals, fat 1.1g, saturates 0.2g, carbs 34.3g, sugars 2.3g, fibre 6.9g, protein 5.6g, salt 0.3g

Porridge bread

Porridge eaters in the house? Use up cold porridge leftovers to make this easy porridge bread. Enjoy with butter and marmalade or with soup and sandwiches.

 PREP 25 mins + proving COOK 45 mins   MAKES 1 loaf (cuts into 8–10 slices)

- 200g cold leftover porridge
- 500g strong white bread flour, plus extra for dusting
- ½ tbsp caster sugar
- 1 tsp flaked sea salt
- 7g dried yeast
- small handful oats, to sprinkle

1 Put the porridge in a large mixing bowl with 300ml lukewarm water. Stir in the flour, sugar, salt and yeast until fully combined. Cover with a damp tea towel and leave to prove for 1 hr, or until it has almost doubled in size.

2 Tip the dough onto a well floured surface and knock the dough back, punching and kneading it – don't worry if it's very soft. Shape the loaf and put it in a non-stick 900g loaf tin. Cover with the damp tea towel and let it prove for another 45 mins. It should expand to fill the tin. Heat the oven to 220C/200C fan/gas 6.

3 Make a slash along the length of the dough and sprinkle on the oats. Bake for 10 mins, then turn the heat down to 190C/170C fan/gas 3 and cook for 30 mins. Turn the loaf out and tap the bottom. If it sounds hollow, then it's ready. If not, put it back in for 5 mins. If any oats fell off when you turned it over, scatter them back over the loaf. Turn out onto a wire rack and leave to cool.

Nutrition per slice (10)
energy 212 kcals, fat 2g, saturates 1g, carbs 41g, sugars 2g, fibre 2g, protein 7g, salt 0.5g

Slow cooker bread

Make an easy loaf with this slow cooker bread recipe. This simple project is perfect for beginners and uses strong wholemeal or white flour.

 PREP 15 mins + proving COOK 2 hours   MAKES 1 loaf (cuts into 10 slices)

- 500g strong wholemeal or white bread flour (or a mix of flours), plus extra for dusting
- 7g sachet fast-action dried yeast
- 1g fine sea salt

1 Mix the flour, yeast and salt and make a well in the middle. Measure 350ml warm water and pour most of it into the well. Mix together with your fingers or a wooden spoon until it forms a slightly wet, pillowy, workable dough – add a splash more water if needed.

2 Knead a lightly floured surface for at least 10 mins until smooth and elastic. This can be done in a stand mixer with a dough hook.

3 Shape into a large, tight ball and sit the ball on a square of parchment. Use this to lift the dough into your slow cooker, cover and set the slow cooker to high. Leave for 2 hrs.

4 Lift the bread out using the parchment. The bottom should be crusty and the top springy, not soft (a digital cooking thermometer inserted into the middle of the loaf should be 90C.) If it isn't ready, return for 15 mins and test again – it could take up to 2 hrs 30 mins.

5 The bread won't get a significant crust or golden colour. Once cooked, you can leave it to cool or put in the oven at 240C/220C fan/gas 9 for 5–10 mins to get some colour.

Nutrition per slice
energy 179 kcals, fat 1g. saturates 0g, carbs 32g, sugars 1g, fibre 5g, protein 8g, salt 0.5g

Brioche loaf

Try homemade brioche with jam or butter for breakfast. It takes a little effort, but the results of this sweet, soft bread are well worth it.

 PREP 40 mins + proving COOK 35 mins   SERVES 8

- 450g strong white bread flour
- 2 tsp fine sea salt
- 50g caster sugar
- 7g dried yeast
- 100ml full-fat milk, at hand-hot temperature
- 4 eggs, room temperature, beaten, plus 1 for egg wash
- 190g salted butter, cubed and softened

1 Put the flour in a stand mixer bowl. Add the salt to one side and sugar and yeast to the other. Mix each side into the flour with your hands, then mix it all together with the dough hook. Add the milk and mix on medium. Gradually add the eggs and mix for 10 mins.

2 Add the butter, 1 or 2 cubes at a time, this will take 5–8 mins. Scrape the dough down the sides, cover and leave for 1½–2 hrs until doubled in size. Put in the fridge for 1 hr.

3 Line a 900g loaf tin with parchment. Divide the dough into 7 equal pieces (weigh it). Lightly flour a work surface, take each piece of dough and pull the corners into the middle, push down and roll into ball.

4 Put the balls into the tin, 4 on one side and 3 in the gaps on the other side. Cover and prove for 30–35 mins or until almost doubled in size. Heat the oven to 180C/160C fan/gas 4. Brush with the egg and bake for 30–35 mins until golden and risen. Cool in the tin for 20 mins, then remove and cool completely.

Nutrition per serving
energy 460 kcals, fat 23g, saturates 14g, carbs 49g, sugars 7g, fibre 2g, protein 12g, salt 1.8g

Brioche burger buns

This brioche dough is very sticky, but don't be tempted to add more flour at first as kneading will bring it together. Serve the buns split and filled with barbecued meat.

 PREP 15 mins + proving COOK 20 mins   MAKES 16 small or 12 large buns

- 2 tsp dried yeast
  (not fast-action)
- 3 tbsp warm milk
- 2 tbsp golden caster sugar
- 450g strong white bread flour,
  plus extra for dusting
- 1 tsp salt
- 4 tbsp unsalted butter, softened
- 2 large eggs, plus 1 beaten
  egg, for glazing
- sesame seeds, for sprinkling

1 Mix 250ml warm water, the yeast, milk and sugar in a bowl. Let stand for 5 mins until frothy. Tip the flour and salt in a bowl with the butter and rub together with your fingertips until it resembles fine breadcrumbs.

2 Make a well in the centre, add the yeast and eggs and use your hands to mix to a sticky dough. Tip out onto a floured work surface and knead for 10 mins by stretching. It's ready when it feels soft and bouncy. Place in an oiled bowl, cover with cling film and set aside for 1–3 hrs until doubled in size.

3 Knock the air out and knead again for 2 mins. The dough should be much less sticky now, but add a little flour if it needs it.

4 Divide into 12 to 16 pieces. Roll into balls and arrange on lined baking sheets. Loosely cover with oiled cling film and leave for 1 hr or until doubled. Heat the oven to 200C/180C fan/ gas 6. Put a shallow baking tray at the bottom.

5 Brush the buns with egg and sprinkle over the seeds. Pour a cup of water into the hot tray to create steam. Bake for 20 mins until golden.

Nutrition per bun (16)
energy 163 kcals, fat 6g, saturates 2g, carbs 22g, sugars 3g, fibre 1g, protein 5g, salt 0.3g

Simit bread

• •

Simit breads are sesame bread rings, sometimes referred to as 'Turkish bagels'. They are sold on every street corner in Turkey and are a classic for breakfast or as a snack.

 PREP 30 mins + proving COOK 15 mins   MAKES 4

- 250g strong white bread flour
- 1 tsp salt
- 1 tsp caster sugar
- 1 tsp (5g) fast-action dried yeast
- 100g sesame seeds
- 1 tbsp pomegranate molasses or molasses syrup

1 Mix the flour, salt and sugar with the yeast and 150ml warm water. Knead for a few mins to a soft dough. Tip onto your work surface and knead for 10–12 mins until the dough is stretchy. Return to a clean bowl, cover and leave for an hour or two until doubled in size.

2 Toast the sesame seeds in a dry frying pan until golden. Set aside in the pan. Mix the molasses with 50ml water in a shallow bowl.

3 Divide the dough into 4 pieces. Roll each into a sausage about 45cm long. Flip the rope of dough back on itself then twist the 2 strands and loop into a ring, squeezing the ends together to secure. Dip each piece into the molasses water, turning to coat, then into the seeds, so each one is well covered. Transfer to a baking tray, cover and leave for 45 mins– 1 hr. Heat the oven to 200C/180C fan/gas 6.

4 When the breads have puffed up, uncover and bake for 15–18 mins until golden. Cool, then wrap in a tea towel to keep them fresh. Can be made up to a day ahead and warmed gently before serving.

• •

Nutrition per simit
energy 408 kcals, fat 15g, saturates 3g, carbs 52g, sugars 4g, fibre 5g, protein 14g, salt 1.2g

Red onion & Gruyère fougasse

This flat, round fougasse loaf is very popular all over France and is a cousin of the Italian focaccia.

 PREP 30 mins + proving COOK 20 mins   MAKES 2 (each serving 3–4)

- 1 red onion, finely sliced
- 1 tbsp olive oil, plus a little extra
- few rosemary sprigs, ½ chopped, ½ broken into 3 or 4 needle pieces
- 100g Gruyère, cubed
- coarse sea salt

FOR THE DOUGH

- 500g strong white bread flour, plus extra for dusting
- 7g sachet fast-action dried yeast
- 2 tsp salt
- 1 tsp sugar
- 2 tbsp olive oil

1 Tip the flour into a bowl, stir in the yeast, then the salt and sugar. Add 400ml hand-hot water and the oil. Mix quickly using your hands to make a soft, slightly sticky dough.

2 Sprinkle the work surface with flour, tip out the dough and knead for about 10 mins until smooth. Put it back in the bowl, cover and leave to rest for 1 hr or until the dough springs back when you press it with your finger.

3 Cook the onion in the oil for 5 mins until soft. Tip the dough onto a lightly floured surface and lightly knead in the onion and chopped rosemary. Cut the dough in half. Roll and press out into 20cm x 25cm rectangles and transfer to a lined baking sheet. Make a large diagonal cut across the centre of each almost to the ends. Make 3 smaller diagonal cuts either side to create a leaf shape.

4 Stick Gruyère and rosemary all over the dough and sprinkle with a little flour and sea salt. Heat the oven to 240C/220C fan/gas 8. Leave the loaves to prove for 20 mins then bake for 13–15 mins until golden.

Nutrition per serving
energy 322 kcals, fat 11g, saturates 4g, carbs 49g, sugars 2g, fibre 2g, protein 11g, salt 1.96g

Chapter 2

SOURDOUGH BREADS

· ·

This collection of recipes is based on using a sourdough starter. From a classic loaf to sourdough hot cross buns, these breads are more time consuming than a classic dry yeasted loaf but are incredibly rewarding. You are left with a slightly chewier, robust and acidic bake, which is completely delicious. Once you get in the swing of it, it's a therapeutic and highly addictive way of baking.

Sourdough starter

Learn how to make a bubbling sourdough starter. After feeding it for 5 days, you can use it to make a levain and then a sourdough loaf.

 PREP 5 days  ENOUGH FOR 2 loaves

- 250g strong white bread flour, preferably organic or stoneground

Day 1:
To begin your starter, mix 50g flour with 50ml tepid water in a jar or, better still, a plastic container. Leave, semi-uncovered, at room temperature for 24 hrs.

Day 2:
Mix 50g flour with 50ml tepid water and stir into yesterday's mixture. Leave, as before, for another 24 hrs.

Day 3:
Repeat day 2.

Day 4:
You should start to see some activity in the mixture now; some bubbles forming and bubbling on top. Repeat day 2.

Day 5:
The mixture should be very active now and ready for making your levain. If it's not, continue to feed daily until it is. When it's ready, it should smell like yogurt.

You now have a starter – the base for bread. Keep it in the fridge (it will stay dormant).

Levain

You can use a levain as the base for a sourdough recipe or to make other recipes such as flatbread, which don't need any more proving time.

 PREP 10 mins + 8 hrs resting   ENOUGH FOR 2 loaves

• 1 quantity sourdough starter
(see page 40)

TO FEED THE STARTER

• 100g strong white bread flour,
preferably organic or
stoneground, plus more if
you need it

FOR THE LEVAIN

• 100g strong white bread flour,
preferably organic or
stoneground, plus more if
you need it

24 hrs before using:

Pour half the starter off and discard. Feed the remainder with 100g flour and 100ml water. Leave it at room temperature and it should become active again – the warmer your room, the quicker this will happen. If your container is transparent, you can mark the outside – the starter will expand, rising above the mark. The longer the starter has been dormant, the more times it will need to be halved and fed to reactivate. Test it by putting a teaspoonful of the mixture in warm water. It should float.

To make the levain, mix 1 tbsp of the starter with 100g flour and 100ml water (this is the same process as feeding the starter, but you should do this in a new, separate bowl, keeping the original starter as back-up in the fridge). The levain is the mixture you'll use to bake your bread. Leave the levain for 8 hrs at room temperature until it becomes active and expands. When ready, a teaspoonful of the mixture should float in warm water.

White sourdough loaf

. . . .

Master the art of sourdough with this step-by-step recipe. You need to make the levain
before you start. Read the introduction to learn how to knead and shape the bread.

 PREP 40 mins + proving/chilling COOK 40 mins   MAKES 2 loaves (cuts into 12-15 slices)

- 1 quantity levain (see page 42)
- 1kg strong white bread flour,
  preferably organic or
  stoneground, plus extra
  for dusting
- 20g fine sea salt

1 Pour 600ml tepid water into the levain and
   mix. Mix in the flour with a rubber spatula to a
   rough dough. Cover and leave somewhere
   warm for at least 30 mins or up to 4 hrs.

2 Sprinkle over the salt and add 50g water to
   the dough. Pinch and scrunch the salt and
   water through the dough with your hands. If
   the dough goes stringy, keep working it until
   it's smooth. Leave for 15 mins.

3 Knead the dough following the steps in the
   introduction on page 7, then leave as
   instructed for 2–3 hrs.

4 Dust 2 bread-proving baskets generously with
   flour. Shape the loaves following the method
   on page 8, then put in the baskets, seam-side
   up and chill overnight.

5 Heat the oven to 240C/220C fan/gas 9. Tip
   the dough onto a lightly floured tray, shape
   and tip into a bread tin or follow the casserole
   method on page 9. Slash the top of the loaf
   with a lame or very sharp knife to create an
   'ear' (see page 8). Bake for 40 mins or until
   golden brown with a well-formed crust.

. . . .

Nutrition per slice (12)
energy 171 kcals, fat 1g, saturates 0.1g, carbs 35g, sugars 0.2g, fibre 1g, protein 6g, salt 0.8g

Sourdough foccacia

Bake a fresh batch of sourdough foccacia with our step-by-step recipe and top breadmaking tips. Enjoy a golden brown slice, drizzled with olive oil.

 PREP 20 MINS + proving COOK 30 mins   SERVES 8-10

- 100g very active sourdough starter (see page 40)
- 500g strong white bread flour
- 15g sea salt flakes
- 4 tbsp olive oil

1 Stir 400ml tepid water into the starter. Add the flour and mix to a rough dough. Cover and leave to rest for at least 30 mins or up to 1 hr.

2 Scatter 10g salt over the dough and scrunch it through with a wet hand. Cover and leave for 20–30 mins, then knead following the instructions on page 7. Prove for 2–3 hrs until risen by about 40 per cent, bubbly and soft.

3 Drizzle a deep 20cm x 30cm baking tray with half the oil and scrape in the dough. Mix the oil into the dough by stretching and folding it on the tray until it comes together in an oily mass. Prove at room temperature for 3–4 hrs or for up to 18 hrs in the fridge.

4 Heat the oven to 220C/200C fan/gas 7. Use your fingers to stretch the dough so it fits into the tray, then dimple the surface with your fingertips. Drizzle with 1 tbsp olive oil and scatter over the remaining salt. Bake for 25–30 mins until puffed up and golden. Drizzle with the remaining oil, then leave to cool for at least 40 mins before cutting into squares.

Nutrition per serving (10)
energy 242 kcals, fat 5g, saturates 1g, carbs 42g, sugars 1g, fibre 2g, protein 7g, salt 1.48g

Sourdough hot cross buns

You can speed the final proving up on these buns by leaving them somewhere a little warm for 2–3 hours but they will have a better shape and flavour if left overnight.

 PREP 40 mins + proving/overnight chilling COOK 25 mins   MAKES 12

- 300g very active sourdough starter (see page 40)
- 2 large eggs, beaten
- 200ml milk
- 500g strong white bread flour, plus extra for dusting
- 60g golden caster sugar
- 1 tsp ground cinnamon
- 1 tsp mixed spice
- 1 orange, zested
- 150g raisins, or a mixture of small dried fruits (such as raisins, mixed peel and cranberries)
- 100g unsalted butter, softened
- 1 tsp salt

1 Mix 200g of the starter in a bowl with most of the egg, the milk, flour, sugar, cinnamon, mixed spice, orange zest and raisins until you have a shaggy dough. Alternatively, do this in a stand mixer fitted with a dough hook. Cover and prove for 30 mins.

2 Work the butter and salt into the dough by squashing it in with your hands. Knead gently for 5 mins until smooth. Return to the bowl, cover and prove for 3–4 hrs until almost doubled in size.

3 Tip the dough onto a floured work surface, knead briefly and divide into 12. Roll each into a ball and put on a baking tray lined with parchment, spacing them a little apart. Cover and leave in the fridge overnight.

4 Remove from the fridge 1 hr before baking. Heat the oven to 200C/180C fan/gas 6. Brush the buns with the remaining egg. Tip the remaining starter into a piping and pipe crosses onto the buns. Bake for 20–25 mins until light brown. Best eaten on the day, but will keep for 2 days in an airtight container.

Nutrition per bun
energy 343 kcals, fat 9g, saturates 5g, carbs 55g, sugars 14g, fibre 2g, protein 9g, salt 0.09g

Sweet sourdough

Enjoy baking sourdough bread? Try this enriched sourdough, which you can make into a brioche loaf or use to create other sweet sourdough bakes.

 PREP 40 mins + proving/chilling COOK 35 mins   MAKES 1–2 loaves (cuts into 20 slices)

- 200g very active sourdough starter (see page 40)
- 3 eggs, beaten
- 1 heaped tsp salt
- 125ml milk
- 500g strong white bread flour, plus extra for dusting
- 60g golden caster sugar or light brown soft sugar
- 100g unsalted butter, softened

1 Tip the starter, most of the egg (reserving a little if you want to glaze it later) and all the other ingredients, except the butter, into a bowl. Mix with your hands to form a rough dough or use a stand mixer with a dough hook. Leave covered for 30 mins.

2 Tip the dough onto a clean work surface and knead for 15–20 mins by hand, or 5–8 mins in a mixer on a medium speed, until springy and glossy. Work the butter into the dough – this will take about 5 mins. At first, it will look messy but keep going until it is smooth and glossy. Cover and leave for 2–3 hrs until nearly doubled in size.

3 For a plaited loaf, chill the dough for an hour to stiffen, split into 3, roll into equal lengths and neatly plait together. Lift onto a lined baking tray, cover and leave in the fridge overnight until the dough has doubled in size.

4 To bake, heat the oven to 200C/180C fan/ gas 6. Brush the top of the loaves with the egg and bake for 30–35 mins until golden.

Nutrition per slice
energy 173 kcals, fat 5g, saturates 3g, carbs 26g, sugars 3g, fibre 1g, protein 5g, salt 0.34g

Rye sourdough starter

This recipe is for a rye sourdough starter, which is a malty flavoured base to sourdough bread. You need to allow 6 days before you can use it for baking.

 PREP 6 days  ENOUGH FOR 2 loaves

FOR THE STARTER
• 250g wholemeal rye flour

Day 1:
To begin your starter, mix 50g of the flour with 50ml tepid water in a jar or, better still, a plastic container. Make sure all the flour is incorporated and leave, covered with a tea towel, at room temperature for 24 hrs.

Days 2, 3, 4 & 5:
Mix 25g flour with 25ml tepid water and stir into yesterday's mixture. Make sure all the flour is incorporated and leave, covered with a tea towel, at room temperature for 24 hrs.

Day 6:
The mix should be really bubbly and giving off a strong smell of alcohol. A teaspoonful of the starter should float in warm water if ready. If not, continue adding 25g flour and 25ml tepid water into the mixture daily until it becomes active. If your jar is becoming full, spoon half the mix out of the jar and continue. Keep your starter in the fridge (it will stay dormant) and 12 hrs before you want to use it, spoon half of it off and feed it with 100g flour and 100ml water. Leave, covered, at room temperature.

Rye sourdough

• •

The malty flavour of rye works well with smoked fish, cured meats or smashed avocado.
For a deeper flavour, chill in the tin overnight, removing an hour before baking.

 PREP 1 hr + proving/cooling COOK 55 mins   MAKES 1 loaf (cuts into 12–15 slices)

- 100g very active rye sourdough starter (see page 52)
- 500g wholemeal rye flour, plus extra for dusting
- 10g fine salt
- 25g butter, softened, for the tin

1 Mix the starter with 400ml tepid water. Whisk or rub together with your hands, not worrying if there are a few lumps. Add the flour and bring into a thick, sticky dough. Cover and leave at room temperature for 2 hrs.

2 Work the salt into the dough then leave, covered, for another 2 hrs.

3 Heavily butter a 900g loaf tin. Dust the work surface with rye flour, then scrape the dough out. Mould into a block roughly the same size as the tin and sit in the tin. Scatter the top with flour. Leave, uncovered, for 2 hrs until risen by about a quarter and craggy on top.

4 Heat the oven to 230/210C fan/gas 8 with a shelf in the middle and a shelf below with a roasting tray on it. Put the loaf on the middle tray and pour a glass of water into the tray. Cook for 50–55 mins until hollow sounding when tapped. (The middle will read 98C on a digital thermometer.) Remove from the tin and cool on a wire rack for at least 4 hrs. This keeps for 3–4 days in an airtight container.

• •

Nutrition per slice (12)
energy 180 kcals, fat 2g, saturates 1g, carbs 33g, sugars 1g, fibre 7g, protein 4g, salt 0.86g

Sourdough pizza

Make homemade sourdough pizza with a wonderfully chewy crust by using a large ovenproof frying pan and the grill rather than your oven.

 PREP 1 hr + chilling COOK 1 hr   MAKES 6

- 1 quantity white sourdough dough (see page 44)
- strong or plain flour, for dusting

FOR THE TOPPING
- 2 x 400g cans plum tomatoes, drained
- 2 tbsp extra virgin olive oil, plus extra to serve
- 1 tsp dried oregano
- 300g mozzarella, torn into chunks
- small bunch basil, leaves picked (optional)

1 Make a batch of white sourdough, following the recipe to the end of step 3. When the dough is ready, tip it onto a lightly floured work surface and divide into 6 pieces. Roll into balls and leave to rest on a floured tray, covered, in the fridge for at least 4 hrs, and up to 18 hrs for a more sour taste.

2 Mix the tomatoes, oil, oregano and a generous pinch of salt. Scrunch everything together with your fingers for a chunky sauce or blitz for a smooth sauce. Chill until needed.

3 Heat a grill to high. On a floured surface, push and stretch a ball of dough into roughly the same size as your ovenproof frying pan. Heat the pan on the hob until very hot, then drape the pizza into the pan, working quickly and carefully. Spread over some of the sauce, a handful of mozzarella and basil, if using.

4 Cook for 2 mins, until little bubbles appear, then put the pan under the grill for another 2–4 mins until the sides are puffed up and the cheese has melted. Drizzle with a little olive oil. Repeat with the remaining dough.

Nutrition per pizza
energy 502 kcals, fat 15g, saturates 8g, carbs 69g, sugars 5g, fibre 4g, protein 21g, salt 2.3g

Chapter 3

FLATBREAD, CHAPATI, ROTI & NAAN

....

These are the breads we turn to for filling, rolling, dunking and scooping – they are easier and quicker to make, and less time consuming, than a traditional yeasted loaf. This chapter ranges from authentic Indian breads to super speedy flatbread you can throw together in less than 30 mins.

Naan bread

Cook your own Indian flatbread at home and you'll never go back to buying them. This is a soft dough. You may need to add more flour or water to get the texture right.

 PREP 20 mins + proving COOK 35 mins   SERVES 6–8

- 7g sachet fast-action dried yeast
- 2 tsp golden caster sugar
- 300g strong white bread flour, plus extra for dusting
- ½ tsp salt
- ½ tsp baking powder
- 25g butter or ghee, melted, plus an extra 2–3 tbsp for the tray and brushing
- 150ml natural yogurt
- 1 tbsp nigella seeds

1 Mix 125ml warm water, the yeast and 1 tsp of the sugar and leave for 10–15 mins or until frothy. Mix the flour, remaining sugar, salt and baking powder. Add the melted butter, yogurt, nigella seeds and yeast mixture. Stir well, then bring the mixture together with your hands to make a very soft dough.

2 Knead first in the bowl, then on a well-floured surface, for 10 mins until smooth and elastic. Shape into a ball, put in a buttered bowl, cover and leave for 1 hr until doubled in size.

3 Divide the dough into 6 balls, put on a tray dusted with flour and cover with a damp cloth. Heat a heavy frying pan over a high heat. Roll each ball out to form a teardrop shape about 21cm long and around 13cm at the widest part. Lay each naan in the pan, let it dry fry and puff up for 3 mins, then cook the other side for another 3–4 mins or until cooked through and charred in patches.

4 Brush with a little butter and cover with foil. Keep warm in the oven and stack on top of each other as you cook them.

Nutrition per serving (8)
energy 224 kcals, fat 8g, saturates 4g, carbs 31g, sugars 3g, fibre 1g, protein 6g, salt 0.4g

Classic flatbread

Make our easiest ever flatbread recipe with just a handful of ingredients. They're perfect for mopping up a warming curry or saucy shakshuka.

 PREP 20 mins + proving COOK 15 mins   MAKES 6

- 110g self-raising flour, plus extra for dusting
- 110g plain wholemeal flour or atta flour
- 3 tbsp rapeseed oil, plus extra for the bowl
- small knob butter, melted

1 Sift the flours and 1 tsp salt into a large bowl. Add 1 tbsp of the oil and 150ml warm water. Bring together into a soft but not too sticky dough (you may need up to 175ml water). If it feels too wet, add some flour. If it's too dry, add water.

2 Tip onto a floured surface and knead for 4–5 mins, or until smooth. Put the dough in an oiled bowl, cover and leave for 30 mins.

3 Tip the dough onto a floured surface. Divide into 6 balls and roll each out into a thin, 18–20cm wide circle using a rolling pin. If you prefer, you can divide again into 12 balls to make smaller flatbreads.

4 Brush a heavy-based pan with oil and cook one flatbread over a high heat for 1–2 mins on each side, or until golden and starting to puff. Put on a plate and brush with butter. Repeat with the rest of the dough.

Nutrition per flatbread
energy 204 kcals, fat 9g, saturates 1g, carbs 26g, sugars 0g, fibre 3g, protein 4g, salt 1g

Triangular bread thins

Bake these easy bread thins with wholemeal spelt and top with smoked salmon, cheese or your favourite ingredients.

 PREP 8 mins COOK 12 mins   MAKES 6

- 190g plain wholemeal spelt flour, plus extra for dusting
- ½ tsp bicarbonate of soda
- 1 tsp baking powder
- 75ml live natural yogurt made up to 150ml with cold water

1 Heat the oven to 200C/180C fan/gas 6 and line a baking sheet with parchment. Mix the flour, bicarbonate of soda and baking powder in a bowl, then stir in the diluted yogurt with the blade of a knife until you have a soft, sticky dough, adding a little water if the mix is dry.

2 Tip the dough onto a lightly floured surface and shape and flatten with your hands to make a 20cm round. Take care not to over-handle the dough as it can make the bread tough. Lift onto the baking sheet and cut into 6 triangles, slightly easing them apart with the knife. Bake the triangles for about 10–12 mins – they don't have to be golden, but should feel firm.

3 Leave to cool on a wire rack. Any leftovers can be packed into a food bag to use later in the week, or frozen until needed.

Nutrition per triangle
energy 115 kcals, fat 1g, saturates 0.3g, carbs 21g, sugars 1g, fibre 2g, protein 5g, salt 0.4g

Quick & puffy flatbread

Whip up these speedy flatbreads for an Indian-style feast. They're like a cheat's version of naan bread, and are great for mopping up a curry.

 PREP 10 mins COOK 15 mins   MAKES 4 large or 6–8 small

- 300g self-raising flour, plus extra for dusting
- ½ tsp baking powder
- 150g natural yogurt
- 1 tbsp vegetable oil
- 1 tsp salt
- melted ghee or butter, for brushing
- cumin seeds, chopped garlic cloves, chopped coriander or chopped chillies (optional)

1 Combine the flour, baking powder, yogurt and oil with 1 tsp salt and 2 tbsp water, and bring together into a rough dough. Tip onto a lightly floured surface and knead for a few minutes until slightly smooth, then divide into 4 to 8 pieces, depending on the size of flatbread you want.

2 Heat a heavy-based frying pan over a high heat. To make basic flatbread, roll the dough pieces out on a lightly floured surface into rough ovals, then fry for 1–2 mins on each side until golden and slightly charred in spots. Alternatively, roll the dough pieces out, brush with a little melted ghee or butter, and scatter over the cumin seeds, garlic, coriander or chillies, if you like. Fold each piece of dough over on itself, then roll out again into a rough oval and cook in the same way.

3 Brush the flatbreads with a little melted butter or ghee, then serve.

Nutrition per serving
energy 328 kcals, fat 5g, saturates 1g, carbs 60g, sugars 3g, fibre 3g, protein 9g, salt 2.1g

Sesame flatbread

These simple flatbread are an impressive addition to any sharing platter. They're surprisingly easy to cook and need just a handful of ingredients.

 PREP 25 mins COOK 45 mins   MAKES 6

- 300g self-raising flour, plus extra for dusting
- 1 tsp salt
- 250g natural yogurt
- 4 tbsp sesame seeds
- 1–2 tbsp vegetable oil

1 Tip the flour into a large bowl and add the salt. Add the yogurt, 2 tbsp water and the sesame seeds, then mix to make a dough (it'll be quite wet). Flour the work surface and tip out the dough. Divide into 6 pieces. Working with 1 ball at a time, and keeping the others covered with a tea towel, roll into flatbread about ½cm thick.

2 Heat a large griddle or frying pan until it is really hot. Brush a flatbread with oil, then put in the pan, oil-side down. Cook for 2–3 mins each side until bubbles appear on the surface and the underneath is brown. Turn over and cook for another 2 mins, then transfer to a plate. Continue cooking the remaining flatbread. Wrap them in foil and keep warm in a low oven until ready to serve, or serve at room temperature.

Nutrition per flatbread
energy 265 kcals, fat 7g, saturates 2g, carbs 41g, sugars 3g, fibre 3g, protein 8g, salt 1.3g

Chapati

Who can resist a warm chapati with your favourite curry. This traditional Indian side dish is easier than you think.

 PREP 15 mins COOK 10 mins   MAKES 10

- 140g wholemeal flour
- 140g plain flour, plus extra for dusting
- 1 tsp salt
- 2 tbsp olive oil, plus extra for greasing

1 In a large bowl, stir together the flours and salt. Use a wooden spoon to stir in the olive oil and enough hot water (about 180ml) to make a soft dough that is elastic but not sticky.

2 Knead the dough on a lightly floured surface for 5–10 mins until it is smooth. Divide into 10 pieces, or less if you want bigger breads. Roll each piece into a ball. Let rest for a few mins.

3 Heat a frying pan over medium heat until hot, and grease lightly. On a lightly floured surface, use a floured rolling pin to roll out the balls of dough until very thin like a tortilla.

4 When the pan starts smoking, put a chapati on it. Cook until the underside has brown spots, about 30 seconds, then flip and cook on the other side. Put on a plate and keep warm while you cook the rest of the chapati.

Nutrition per serving
energy 121 kcals, fat 3g, saturates 0.4g, carbs 20g, sugars 0.3g, fibre 2g, protein 3g, salt 0.5g

Roti

Try these easy flatbreads, which originate from the Indian subcontinent. They are perfect for scooping up sauce.

 PREP 10 mins + resting COOK 10 mins   SERVES 6

- 115g self-raising flour
- 115g wholemeal flour
- 1½ tsp salt
- 3 tbsp vegetable oil, plus extra for frying
- 2 tsp butter, for frying

1 Sift both flours and salt into a large mixing bowl. Add 1 tbsp of the oil and 175–200ml warm water and bring together to make a soft but not too sticky dough. If it feels a little wet, add a bit more flour.

2 Tip the dough onto a lightly floured worktop and knead for 4–5 mins or until smooth and elastic. Set aside in a lightly oiled bowl for 30 mins.

3 Divide the dough into 6 equal-sized pieces (weigh each piece for accuracy if you like). Using a rolling pin roll each one into a thin circle about 18–20cm wide.

4 Heat a little of the remaining oil and butter in a heavy-based pan over a high heat. Once foaming, add the rolled out roti, 1 at a time, and cook for 1–2 mins on each side or until speckled golden brown and beginning to puff up. Set aside on a warm plate until ready to eat.

Nutrition per serving
energy 193 kcals, fat 7g, saturates 1g, carbs 27g, sugars 0.4g, fibre 3g, protein 4g, salt 1.41g

Two-ingredients wholemeal flatbread

These flatbreads are a doddle – simply make a large batch out of storecupboard ingredients and freeze them for later in the week.

 PREP 10 mins COOK 10 mins   MAKES 8

- 350g wholemeal flour, plus extra for dusting
- 4 tsp cold-pressed rapeseed oil

1 Put the flour in a medium bowl and rub in the oil with your fingertips. Stir in 225ml warm water, mix thoroughly, then knead until the dough feels smooth and elastic.

2 Put the dough onto a lightly floured surface and divide into 8 balls. Sprinkle the work surface with a little more flour and roll out one of the balls very thinly, using a floured rolling pin, to around 22cm. Turn the dough regularly and sprinkle with more flour if it begins to stick. Make the other flatbreads in the same way. If making ahead, freeze before cooking.

3 Put a non-slick frying pan over a high heat and, once hot, add one of the flatbreads. Cook for 30 secs, then turn over and cook on the other side for 30 secs. Press the flatbread with a spatula while cooking to encourage it to puff up and cook inside – it should be lightly browned in patches and look fairly dry, without being crisp. Repeat with the rest of the flatbreads, keeping them warm by wrapping in a clean tea towel until needed.

Nutrition per flatbread
energy 168 kcals, fat 2g, saturates 0g, carbs 27g, sugars 1g, fibre 5g, protein 6g, salt 0g

Charred onion & whipped feta flatbread

Top homemade flatbread with whipped feta and charred onions for a sensational lunch or supper. Finish off with a touch of harissa, thyme and honey.

 PREP 25 mins + proving COOK 45 mins   MAKES 4 medium or 6 small flatbread

- 300g strong white bread flour, plus extra for dusting
- 1 tsp salt
- 7g sachet fast-action dried yeast
- 70ml olive oil, plus extra for proving
- ½ tbsp extra virgin olive oil
- 3 onions, cut into chunky wedges
- 5 thyme sprigs, plus extra leaves to serve
- 2 tbsp honey, plus extra to serve
- 100g feta
- 50g thick Greek yogurt
- 1–2 tbsp rose harissa

1 Combine the flour, salt and the yeast in a bowl. Make a well in the centre and tip in 150ml warm water and the olive oil. Mix until combined, then knead on a lightly floured surface for 10 mins. Tip into a lightly oiled bowl, cover and leave to rise for at least 1 hr, or until doubled in size.

2 Heat the oven to 200C/180C fan/gas 6. Heat the extra virgin olive oil in a frying pan over a high heat, and fry the onions for about 5 mins until beginning to char, stirring every so often. Tip into a roasting tin with the thyme and honey. Roast for 15 mins until softened.

3 Crumble the feta into a bowl with the yogurt, then whisk until smooth and creamy.

4 Heat a dry frying pan over a medium heat. Divide the dough into 4 to 6 balls and roll out into 1cm-thick circles on a lightly floured surface. Fry, 1 at a time, for 2 mins on each side until cooked and lightly charred. Top with the feta yogurt, harissa, onions, a bit of extra thyme and honey and a pinch of sea salt.

Nutrition per serving (6)
energy 40 kcals, fat 18g, saturates 5g, carbs 49g, sugars 10g, fibre 3g, protein 10g, salt 1.4g

Lamb & smoky aubergine flatbread

This is loosely based on the Turkish dish of lahmacun, but with a thicker bread base similar to pizza. Great for using leftover lamb, the aubergine gives a smoky depth.

 PREP 30 mins + proving COOK 25 mins   SERVES 2

FOR THE FLATBREAD
- 7g sachet fast-action dried yeast
- 200g '00' flour
- 200g strong white bread flour
- 2 tsp salt
- 1 tbsp olive oil

FOR THE TOPPING
- 1 aubergine
- ½ red onion, finely sliced
- 150g leftover lamb, chopped
- 2 tbsp finely chopped parsley
- 1 tomato, finely chopped
- 1 tbsp tomato purée
- 1 garlic clove, crushed
- pinch ground cumin
- pinch smoked paprika
- 1 tbsp pomegranate molasses (optional)
- 1 tbsp olive oil
- 1 tbsp pine nuts
- 1 tsp tahini

1 Mix the yeast and 250ml warm water in a jug. Leave to sit for a few mins. Sift the flours and salt into a bowl. Slowly stir in the yeast, then the oil. Turn out onto a clean surface. Knead for 5 mins until you have a smooth, springy dough. Return to the bowl, cover with cling film and leave for 30 mins to puff up.

2 Char the aubergine over a gas flame or under a hot grill until smoky and soft enough to pull apart with a fork. Set aside to cool.

3 Tip the dough out and knead for a few mins, then divide into 4 and roll into smooth balls. Wrap 3 in cling film and freeze for later use.

4 Heat the oven to 240C/220C fan/gas 8. Flatten the ball with your palm and roll out into a 25–30cm long base. Place on an oiled baking sheet and leave to rise.

5 Scoop the aubergine into a bowl and mix with the other topping ingredients, apart from the pine nuts and tahini. Spread over the flatbread, then scatter with pine nuts. Bake for 10–12 mins until puffed and golden. Mix the tahini with 1 tbsp water and drizzle over.

Nutrition per serving
energy 711 kcals, fat 28g, saturates 7g, carbs 72g, sugars 10g, fibre 13g, protein 36g, salt 2.1g

Turkish lamb flatbread

Perfect finger food for a party. Put out this spiced lamb flatbread, sliced into squares, and watch it disappear in minutes

 PREP 45 mins + proving COOK 35 mins   SERVES 6-8

- 1 tsp dried yeast
- 400g plain flour, plus extra for dusting
- 1 tsp salt
- 1 onion, finely chopped
- 2 garlic cloves, finely chopped
- 1 tbsp olive oil, plus extra for greasing
- 500g lean lamb mince
- 1 tsp chilli flakes (or 2 tsp Turkish)
- 2 tsp ground cumin
- 2 tsp ground cinnamon
- 4 tbsp tomato purée
- 400g can plum tomatoes
- 4 tbsp pomegranate molasses, plus extra for drizzling
- 1 tsp semolina
- 2 small red onions, thinly sliced
- 50g pine nuts
- 100g feta, crumbled
- 2 tbsp chopped parsley
- 50g pomegranate seeds

1 Mix the yeast with 250ml warm water, then leave for 5–10 mins until foamy. Put the flour and salt in a stand mixer fitted with a dough hook, add the liquid and mix until it comes together into a ball. If too sticky, add 2 tbsp flour and mix again. Knead for 8–10 mins on a high speed until smooth. Put in a lightly oiled bowl, cover and leave until doubled in size.

2 Heat the oven to 240C/220C fan/gas 9. Put a baking sheet on the middle shelf. Fry the onion and garlic in the oil for 10 mins until golden. Add the lamb, brown for 5 mins, then pour off excess oil. Add the spices, tomato purée, drained tomatoes and molasses, season and cook for 5 mins. Cool completely.

3 Roll out the dough on a floured surface to a 30cm x 40cm rectangle. Sprinkle the semolina on a baking sheet and slide on the dough. Spread on the lamb, then the red onion, pine nuts and feta. Put onto the heated baking sheet and cook for 10–15 mins until crisp on the bottom. Drizzle with molasses and scatter over the parsley and pomegranate seeds.

Nutrition per serving (8)
energy 433 kcals, fat 14g, saturates 4g, carbs 52g, sugars 12g, fibre 5g, protein 23g, salt 1.4g

Chapter 4

QUICK BREADS

. . . .

Looking for a bread that cuts out the long rising time? A big drawback for making bread for some is its time-consuming method of multiple stages – in particular the rising and proving. This collection of breads proves that some can take no time at all and you'll still be left with an impressive looking and tasting loaf. From a loaf that uses plain flour to Irish soda bread, perfect for dunking into soups, these recipes are here for days when you're strapped for time.

Courgette & cheddar soda bread

This simple loaf is easy to make but big on flavour and texture, with mature cheese, grated courgettes, oats and thyme.

 PREP 25 mins COOK 40 mins   MAKES 1 loaf (cuts into 12 slices)

- 2 medium courgettes
- 400g self-raising flour, plus extra for dusting
- 50g rolled oats
- 1½ tsp bicarbonate of soda
- 1 tsp fine salt
- 75g mature cheddar, grated
- small bunch thyme, leaves only
- 284ml pot buttermilk
- 1 tbsp clear honey
- 1 egg, beaten

1 Heat the oven to 200C/180C fan/gas 6 and dust a baking sheet with a little flour. Place a box grater on top of a clean tea towel and coarsely grate the courgettes. Lift the corners of the tea towel and, holding it over the sink, twist to compact the courgettes and squeeze out as much liquid as you can.

2 Put the flour, oats, bicarb and salt in a bowl. Add most of the cheddar (save a little for the top), the thyme and the courgette. Mix the buttermilk and honey, then pour into the flour mixture. Stir with a wooden spoon until the dough starts to clump together, then tip onto a work surface and knead briefly to bring all the loose bits together – try not to overwork the dough or the bread will be heavy.

3 Shape into a loaf and place on the baking sheet. Brush with egg and sprinkle with the remaining cheese. Use a sharp knife to score a deep cross on top of the loaf, then bake for 40 mins until deep golden brown. Best served warm, but leftovers will keep for 1–2 days.

Nutrition per serving
energy 185 kcals, fat 4g, saturates 2g, carbs 30g, sugars 3g, fibre 3g, protein 7g, salt 1.2g

Onion soda bread with whipped butter

Perk up homemade soda bread with onion and a light but punchy mustard butter. Serve alongside your favourite cold meats and a fresh salad.

 PREP 20 mins COOK 1 hr  SERVES 8-10 (or 6-8 with leftovers)

- 340g strong wholemeal bread flour
- 340g strong white bread flour, plus extra for dusting
- 2 tsp bicarbonate of soda
- 40g dried onion flakes
- 1 tbsp nigella seeds
- 1½ tsp salt
- 85g butter, melted
- 625ml natural yogurt
- splash milk
- 1 tbsp oats

FOR THE MUSTARD BUTTER

- 135g unsalted butter, chopped and softened
- 25g English mustard

1 Heat the oven to 200C/180C fan/gas 6. Tip the flours into a bowl with the bicarb, onion flakes, nigella seeds and salt. Stir together and make a well in the middle. Tip in the butter and yogurt and bring together into a soft, sticky dough using a spatula. If it seems dry, add a splash of milk.

2 Tip the dough out onto a lightly floured surface and gently form into a round. Lift onto a lightly floured baking sheet, cut a deep cross in the top using a sharp knife and sprinkle over the oats. Bake for 1 hr, or until golden and the loaf sounds hollow when tapped underneath. Cool on a wire rack.

3 While the bread cools, beat the butter, mustard and a pinch of sea salt together until light and airy. Spoon into a small pot. Slice the bread and serve with the mustard butter for spreading over.

Nutrition per serving (10)
energy 485 kcals, fat 22g, saturates 13g, carbs 56g, sugars 6g, fibre 5g, protein 13g, salt 3.1g

Plain flour bread

• •

This no-yeast bread is made using any plain flour you have at home. It's denser than a yeasted bread, but very satisfying spread with butter or dunked in hot soup.

 PREP 10 mins COOK 45 mins   MAKES 1 loaf (cuts into 10 slices)

- 500g plain white or wholemeal flour, plus extra for dusting
- 2 tsp bicarbonate of soda
- ½ tsp fine salt
- 1 tbsp sugar
- 350ml–400ml natural yogurt or buttermilk
- handful oats or seeds (optional)

1 Heat the oven to 200C/180C fan/gas 6 and line a 900g loaf tin with parchment. Put a flat baking sheet in the oven to get really hot.

2 Mix the flour, bicarb, salt and sugar in a large bowl until evenly distributed. Make a well in the centre and tip in the yogurt. Bring together to make a slightly sticky dough.

3 Lightly dust the dough with extra flour and form into a fat log, around the same size as the tin. Put the dough in the tin. Dip a wooden spoon in flour and make a line along the centre. Top with a small handful of oats or seeds, if you like.

4 Bake on the hot baking sheet for 40–45 mins or until golden brown. Leave to cool in the tin, then turn out onto a wire rack to cool completely before cutting into slices.

• •

Nutrition per serving
energy 205 kcals, fat 1g, saturates 0g, carbs 42g, sugars 4g, fibre 2g, protein 6g, salt 0.8g

Rustic bread

• •

This is a traditional Sicilian bread that you can make in the morning to get ahead.

 PREP 15 mins COOK 20 mins   MAKES 8

- 250g strong white bread flour
- 1 tsp fast-action dried yeast
- ½ tsp salt
- 1 tbsp olive oil, plus extra for drizzling
- 200ml sparkling water
- semolina, for sprinkling (optional)
- finely chopped rosemary and flaked sea salt and black pepper, for sprinkling

1 Heat the oven to 220C/fan 200C/gas 7. Mix together the flour, yeast and salt. Add the oil, then pour in the water gradually, adding enough to make a soft dough. Knead the dough on a lightly floured surface for about 4–5 mins until the dough feels strong, bouncy and has a silky feel to it.

2 Cut the dough into 8 pieces, then roll out into rough rounds about 16–17cm in diameter. (Don't pile them on top of each other or they will stick together.)

3 Sprinkle a baking sheet or 2 with semolina if you have it, otherwise leave plain. Lay the breads on the sheets and let them sit for 5 mins, then scatter with rosemary, salt and pepper and drizzle with olive oil. Bake in batches for 8–10 mins until puffy and golden. Can be made 3–4 hrs ahead.

• •

Nutrition per bread
energy 137 kcals, fat 4g, saturates 1g, carbs 24g, sugars 0g, fibre 1g, protein 4g, salt 0.94g

Soda farls

Celebrate St Patrick's Day with soda farls – an Irish soda bread flattened into a circle and divided into four 'farls'. Eat warm with butter.

 PREP 10 mins COOK 20 mins   SERVES 4

- 250g plain flour, plus extra for dusting
- ½ tsp salt
- 1 tsp sugar
- 1 heaped tsp bicarbonate of soda
- 225ml buttermilk

1 Tip the flour into a large bowl and stir through the salt, sugar and bicarb. Make a well in the centre and pour in the buttermilk, then swiftly stir to combine. Tip onto a lightly floured surface and knead briefly. Roll into a roughly 20cm circle and cut into quarters.

2 Heat a skillet or heavy-based frying pan over a low-medium heat. Add the farls and cook for 8–10 mins on each side, or until golden brown and cooked through. Remove from the heat and leave the farls to cool in the pan for 10 mins. Split open and eat warm with butter.

Nutrition per serving
energy 255 kcals, fat 1g, saturates 0.4g, carbs 52g, sugars 4g, fibre 3g, protein 8g, salt 1.4g

Simple soda bread

Want a simple bread recipe? This soda bread requires no kneading or proving, is yeast-free and takes mere minutes to prepare. Above all, it's delicious.

 PREP 5 mins COOK 40 mins  MAKES 1 loaf (cuts into 10 slices)

- 500g plain wholemeal flour
- 2 tsp sea salt
- 1 tsp bicarbonate of soda
- 1 tbsp finely chopped rosemary (optional)
- 400ml full-fat milk
- 1 lemon, juiced
- 2 tsp honey

1 Heat the oven to 200C/180C fan/gas 6. Mix together the flour, salt and bicarb in a bowl. And if you'd like rosemary bread, add the chopped rosemary too.

2 Mix together the milk and lemon juice in a jug and wait for a minute as it magically turns into buttermilk. Then stir in the honey and simply pour it into the flour mixture. Stir it with a knife for a minute until the whole thing comes together into a sticky dough.

3 Tip onto a floured work surface and shape it into a ball. Put the ball on a floured baking tray and, using a sharp knife, make a deep cross on top.

4 Bake for 40 mins. Cool on a wire rack until warm, then slice and serve.

Nutrition per serving
energy 207 kcals, fat 2g, saturates 1g, carbs 36g, sugars 4g, fibre 5g, protein 7g, salt 1.3g

Stout & apple wheaten bread

An easy beer bread with chunks of sweet apple. This wholemeal loaf is made with buttermilk and treacle for a dense, moist slice you can enjoy with your tea.

 PREP 30 mins COOK 40 mins   MAKES 3 loaves

- 60g butter, cut into small cubes, plus more for the tins
- 1 large apple (or 2 small ones), peeled, cored and diced
- 175g plain flour
- 450g wholemeal flour
- 90g medium oatmeal
- 1 tsp salt
- 2½ tsp bicarbonate of soda
- 4 tbsp muscovado sugar
- 175ml good-quality stout
- 5 tbsp treacle
- 400ml buttermilk
- oat flakes, pinhead oatmeal or sesame seeds (or a mixture of all 3), for sprinkling

1 Heat the oven to 180C/160C fan/gas 4. Butter 3 x 450g loaf tins. Toss the apple with 2 tbsp of the plain flour. Mix the flours and oatmeal with 1 tsp salt and the bicarbonate of soda. Add the butter and rub it in with your fingertips. Stir in the sugar.

2 Make a well in the middle of the mixture and gradually pour in the stout, followed by the treacle, then the buttermilk. Mix the liquids in with a butter knife as they are added, also working in the floured apple – work quickly and be careful not to overmix.

3 Divide the mixture between the loaf tins, sprinkle over the oats or seeds, and bake for 35–40 mins. To test whether the loaves are ready, remove one from the tin and tap the bottom. If it sounds hollow, it's ready; if not, return to the oven for a little longer. Turn the loaves out of the tins and leave to cool on a wire rack.

Nutrition per serving
energy 126 kcals, fat 2g, saturates 1g, carbs 22g, sugars 7g, fibre 2g, protein 3g, salt 0.5g

Einkorn soda bread

Use einkorn flour – one of the earliest forms of wheat eaten by humankind – to make this soda bread. It delivers a lovely rich and nutty flavour.

PREP 10 mins COOK 45 mins SERVES 8–10

- 250g einkorn flour, plus extra for dusting
- 250g plain flour
- 2 tsp bicarbonate of soda
- 1½ tsp fine sea salt
- 1 tbsp soft brown sugar
- 370ml natural yogurt
- 1 large egg

1 Heat the oven to 200C/180C fan/gas 6. Sprinkle a little of the einkorn flour over a baking sheet, then tip both flours, the bicarbonate of soda, salt and sugar into a bowl and stir to combine. Whisk the yogurt and egg together in a jug.

2 Make a well in the centre of the dry ingredients and pour in the wet mixture. Swiftly mix the ingredients together to create a slightly sticky dough. Form into a round, about 4–5cm thick and put in the middle of the baking sheet. Dip the handle of a wooden spoon into some flour, then lightly press into the top to create a cross. Lightly dust with a little more einkorn flour.

3 Bake in the oven for 40–45 mins or until slightly risen with no grey, uncooked patches in the cross. Set aside to cool, then serve with salted butter, if you like.

Nutrition per serving (10)
energy 225 kcals, fat 3g, saturates 1g, carbs 40g, sugars 5g, fibre 3g, protein 8g, salt 1.4g

Chapter 5

FOCACCIA & PIZZA

Focaccia and pizza are both traditional breads in their own right, originating from Italy. Focaccia is a rich, spongy loaf made using extra virgin olive oil and often flavoured with herbs like rosemary and thyme or topped with caramelized onion, olives or lemon. Pizza has a yeasted base and is topped with a tomato sauce and cheese, as well as a range of other toppings. Both of these can be made at home with a little effort, but rewarding and delicious results!

Focaccia

Make a simple, homemade version of this classic Italian bread. You can use rosemary or any other woody herbs, such as thyme or sage.

 PREP 25 mins + proving COOK 20 mins SERVES 12

- 500g strong white bread flour, plus extra for dusting
- 7g sachet fast-action dried yeast
- 2 tsp fine sea salt
- 5 tbsp olive oil, plus extra for the tin and to serve
- 1 tsp flaky sea salt
- ¼ small bunch rosemary, sprigs picked

1 Tip the flour into a bowl. Mix the yeast into one side of the flour and the fine salt into the other, then mix together. This initial seperation prevents the salt from killing the yeast.

2 Make a well in the middle. Add 2 tbsp oil and gradually pour in 350–400ml lukewarm water until you have a slightly sticky dough (you may not need all the water). Flour the work surface and tip the dough onto it. Knead for 5–10 mins until soft and less sticky. Put the dough into a clean bowl, cover with a tea towel and leave for 1 hr until doubled in size.

3 Oil a 25cm x 35cm shallow tin. Tip the dough onto the work surface, then stretch it to fill the tin. Cover and leave for 35–45 mins.

4 Heat the oven to 220C/200C fan/gas 7. Press your fingers into the dough to make dimples. Mix together 1½ tbsp olive oil, 1 tbsp water and the flaky salt and drizzle. Push sprigs of rosemary into the dimples in the dough.

5 Bake for 20 mins until golden. Whilst still hot, drizzle over 1–2 tbsp oil. Cut into squares and serve warm or cold with extra olive oil.

Nutrition per serving
energy 208 kcals, fat 7g, saturates 1g, carbs 31g, sugars 0g, fibre 1g, protein 5g, salt 1.2g

Mozzarella-stuffed crust pizza

Create your own cheesy masterpiece at home with our mozzarella pizza that goes the extra mile. You can't beat an oozy stuffed crust.

 PREP 30 mins + proving COOK 35 mins   SERVES 4

- 300g strong white bread flour
- 1 tsp fast-action dried yeast
- ½ tsp golden caster sugar, plus a pinch
- 1 tsp salt
- 3 tbsp olive oil, plus a drizzle
- 200ml milk, at hand-hot temperature
- 250ml passata
- 2 garlic cloves, squashed
- ½ tsp dried oregano
- 1–2 tbsp polenta
- 250g grated mozzarella

1 Combine the flour, yeast, sugar and salt in stand mixer fitted with a dough hook. Add 1½ tbsp oil and the milk and mix, then knead for 5–7 mins until you have a smooth dough. Cover with cling film and leave for 1–2 hrs until doubled in size.

2 Simmer the remaining oil, passata, garlic, oregano and a pinch of sugar in a pan for 5–10 mins until thick. Remove the garlic.

3 Dust the work surface with polenta and tip out the dough. Punch and shape into a disc, then roll to a 35cm circle. Dust a baking sheet with polenta and slide the dough on top. Use half the mozzarella to create a ring around the outside edge, leaving a ½cm gap. Brush water inside the cheese ring, fold the outside edge over the mozzarella and press firmly.

4 Spoon the sauce into the middle, add the rest of the mozzarella and brush the crust with oil. Rest for 30 mins. Heat the oven to 240C/220C fan/gas 9 with a large baking sheet on the middle shelf. Slide the pizza onto the hot tray and cook for 15–20 mins.

Nutrition per serving
energy 573 kcals, fat 23g, saturates 11g, carbs 65g, sugars 6g, fibre 3g, protein 24g, salt 1.9g

Caramelized onion focaccia

Cut this onion focaccia into squares or tear-and-share – it's an ideal side dish for a barbecue alongside summer salads and can be made a day ahead.

 PREP 20 mins + proving COOK 1 hr   SERVES 8-10

- 250g '00' flour
- 250g strong white bread flour
- 7g sachet fast-action dried yeast
- 10g fine sea salt
- 3 tbsp good-quality olive oil, plus extra for the bowl and drizzling
- knob butter
- 3 large red onions, sliced
- 2 tbsp balsamic vinegar
- flaked sea salt

1 Mix the flours with the yeast and salt. Add 1 tbsp oil, then pour in 320ml lukewarm water and mix well. You want a very soft dough – don't worry if it looks a little wet, this will make a lighter focaccia. Knead for 5 mins if using a stand mixer or 10 mins by hand, using a dough scraper if you have one and lightly oiling your hands and the surface. Transfer to a lightly oiled bowl, cover with a damp tea towel and leave until it has doubled in size.

2 Melt the butter in a frying pan with the rest of the oil, onion and a pinch of salt and cook gently for 20 mins until very soft. Pour in the vinegar, cooking for 10 mins until sticky. Cool.

3 Oil an A4-sized roasting tin, scrape in the dough and reshape in the tin, gently pushing into the corners. Scatter over the onions, cover with oiled cling film and leave to puff up.

4 Heat the oven to 220C/200C fan/gas 7. Using your fingers, lightly dimple the dough all over, drizzle with oil and sprinkle with sea salt. Bake for 30 mins until golden. Can be made the day before and stored in an airtight container.

Nutrition per serving (10)
energy 250 kcals, fat 4g, saturates 1g, carbs 44g, sugars 5g, fibre 3g, protein 7g, salt 1g

Salami stromboli

Enjoy a pizza, calzone and focaccia all rolled into one with this stromboli stuffed with salami and mozzarella. It can be made ahead and frozen.

 PREP 30 mins + proving COOK 40 mins   SERVES 4

FOR THE DOUGH
- 400g strong white bread flour, plus extra for dusting
- 5g fast-action dried yeast
- 1 tsp salt
- 1 tbsp olive oil, plus extra for brushing

FOR THE FILLING
- 20 slices Milano salami (about 100g)
- 150g grated mozzarella
- handful basil leaves

1 Tip the flour into a bowl, then stir in the yeast and salt. Pour in 250ml warm water and the oil and bring together with a wooden spoon to make a soft dough. Tip onto a surface and knead for 10 mins until smooth. Put the dough back in the bowl, cover with a tea towel and set aside for 40 mins until doubled in size.

2 Roll the dough out on a lightly floured surface to a 35cm x 20cm rectangle. Layer over the salami (leaving a bit of a border), then scatter over the mozzarella and finally the basil. Tuck the shorter edges in and roll the whole thing up like a Swiss roll. Will keep frozen, tightly wrapped in foil, for up to 1 month. Can either be defrosted and baked or baked from frozen.

3 Leave the loaf to rest for 20 mins on a baking tray. Heat the oven to 200C/180C/gas 6. Brush all over with olive oil and sprinkle with sea salt. Bake for 40 mins until puffed up and golden. If cooking from frozen, bake for 1 hr. Leave to cool for 10 mins before slicing and serving with salad.

Nutrition per serving
energy 570 kcals, fat 19g, saturates 8g, carbs 76g, sugars 1g, fibre 3g, protein 23g, salt 2.4g

Deep-dish meatball marinara pizza

Be inspired by America's deep-dish pizzas and make our meatball marinara version with a lip-smacking sauce. It takes a little effort, but it's well worth it.

 PREP 1 hr + proving COOK 1 hr   SERVES 6

- 500g strong white bread flour, plus extra for dusting
- 1 tsp salt
- 1½ tsp fast-action dried yeast
- ½ tbsp caster sugar, plus 1 tsp for the sauce
- 5 tbsp olive oil, plus extra for greasing
- 250–300ml semi-skimmed milk
- 1 small onion, finely chopped
- 1 garlic clove, crushed
- 400g can chopped tomatoes
- 1 tbsp tomato purée
- 2 tsp dried oregano
- 230g grated mozzarella
- 300g pork mince
- 50g fresh breadcrumbs
- 1 medium egg yolk
- ½ tsp fennel seeds, crushed
- ½ tbsp fine polenta
- 20g Parmesan
- a few leaves oregano

1 Mix the flour, salt, yeast and sugar in a stand mixer fitted with a dough hook. Add ½ tbsp oil and the milk and mix. Knead for 5–7 mins until you have a smooth dough. Cover with cling film and leave for 1–2 hrs until doubled in size.

2 Fry the onion in 1 tbsp olive oil with a large pinch of salt for 12–15 mins. Add the garlic and fry for 1 min more. Stir in the tomatoes, purée, oregano and 1 tsp sugar and simmer for 15–20 mins until the sauce thickens. Season.

3 Roll and stretch the risen dough out over an oiled baking tray, making a lipped crust at the edge. Spread over the sauce and half the mozzarella. Leave to rest for 30 mins.

4 Heat the oven to 240C/220C fan/gas 8 with a baking sheet inside. Mix the pork, crumbs, egg, fennel and seasoning. Roll into 12 balls and brown in the remaining oil for 5 mins.

5 Brush the pizza crust with a little more oil and sprinkle with polenta. Add the meatballs and remaining mozzarella. Slide the pizza tray onto the hot baking sheet and bake for 15–18 mins. Finish with Parmesan and oregano.

Nutrition per serving
energy 686 kcals, fat 28g, saturates 10g, carbs 75g, sugars 8g, fibre 4g, protein 32g, salt 1.7g

Potato & turmeric focaccia

Try this twist on a traditional focaccia with a topping of potato, turmeric and rosemary. It takes a little effort, but you'll be well rewarded for your time.

 PREP 20 mins + overnight proving/resting COOK 30 mins   SERVES 12

- 1 tsp fresh yeast or ½ tsp fast-action dried yeast
- 2 tbsp olive oil
- 450g strong white bread flour
- 1 tsp salt

FOR THE TOPPING

- 3 medium waxy potatoes, thinly sliced
- 2 tbsp olive oil, plus extra for drizzling
- 1 tsp turmeric
- 1 rosemary sprig, leaves picked and chopped

1 In a large bowl, dissolve the yeast in 350ml cold water and add the oil. Add the flour and salt and mix thoroughly with your hands to make a dough. Cover and leave in the fridge or a cool place overnight.

2 The next day, turn your dough out onto an oiled tray, approx 30cm x 20cm. Using your fingertips, gently stretch the dough into a rectangle, then fold it in half. Rotate the dough 90 degrees and repeat the process. Leave to rest for 30 mins. Repeat the stretching, folding and resting process twice more.

3 Heat the oven to 240C/220C fan/gas 9. Gently stretch the dough to fill your tray. If it shrinks back, don't force it – rest for 10 more mins, then try again.

4 Spread the potato slices over the dough, overlapping. Mix the oil with the turmeric and brush over, then sprinkle with sea salt and bake on the top shelf of the oven for 25–30 mins. When cooked, drizzle with a little more olive oil and scatter over the rosemary.

Nutrition per serving
energy 211 kcals, fat 5g, saturates 1g, carbs 36g, sugars 1g, fibre 2g, protein 6g, salt 0.1g

Fig & Serrano ham picnic bread

Enjoy this as it is with extra virgin olive oil and balsamic vinegar for dunking, or smear with soft goat's cheese and top with a handful of rocket.

 PREP 30 mins + proving COOK 30 mins   SERVES 8

- 500g pack bread mix (we used ciabatta)
- 15 sage leaves, 5 finely shredded, the rest left whole
- 1 tsp freshly ground black pepper
- 4 tbsp good-quality olive oil
- 2 garlic cloves, crushed
- plain flour, for dusting
- 4–5 fresh figs, thickly sliced
- ½ onion, sliced as thinly as possible
- 100g Serrano ham slices
- flaked sea salt, for sprinkling

1 Tip the bread mix into a bowl with the shredded sage and pepper. Add 2 tbsp of the oil, the garlic and required amount of water. Stir, then bring the dough together and knead for 5 mins on a floured surface until smooth. Put in a bowl, cover and leave until doubled in size.

2 Punch the dough a few times, then divide into 8 portions. Roll each to a flattish bap shape on a lightly floured surface and arrange in a roughly 20cm x 30cm roasting tin. Toss the whole sage leaves, figs, onion and ham with 1 tbsp of the oil, then scatter these over the top. Use your fingers to press the toppings into the bread a little, and spread the bread to fill any gaps. Cover loosely with oiled cling film and leave for 20 mins until it has puffed up.

3 Heat the oven to 180C/160C fan/gas 4. Drizzle over the remaining oil, sprinkle with sea salt and pepper and bake for 30 mins until risen, golden and crisp. Cool in the tin for 15 mins, then transfer to a wire rack to cool completely.

Nutrition per serving
energy 248 kcals, fat 8g, saturates 2g, carbs 33g, sugars 5g, fibre 2g, protein 10g, salt 1.4g

Pesto focaccia sandwich

The filling for your sandwich is baked into the bread here, making this an easy picnic option. To make it veggie, look for a vegetarian pesto.

 PREP 40 mins + proving COOK 30 mins   SERVES 10-12

- 500g strong white bread flour
- 7g sachet fast-action dried yeast
- 1 tsp salt
- 2 tbsp olive oil, plus extra for drizzling
- small pack basil, leaves picked
- 2 x 125g mozzarella balls
- 2 tbsp pine nuts, toasted
- 3 tbsp green pesto
- flaked sea salt

1 Put the flour, yeast and salt in a bowl, ensuring the yeast and salt don't touch. Pour in 350ml lukewarm water and the oil and bring into a wet, elastic dough. If using a stand mixer, knead for 5 mins or until the dough stops sticking to the bowl. If kneading by hand, knead for 10 mins on a lightly floured surface.

2 Put the dough in a lightly oiled bowl, cover with a damp tea towel and leave for 1 hr until doubled in size. Line a 20cm x 30cm roasting tin with crumpled parchment. Cut the dough in half, lightly press half into the tin and stretch it out to fill. Cover with basil, mozzarella and pine nuts, then spread the other half on top. Cover and leave for 1 hr until light and puffy.

3 Heat the oven to 200C/180C fan/gas 6. Press indents with your fingers into the top of the dough (if the indents bounce back, leave the dough for longer). Fill the indents with pesto, sprinkle with sea salt and drizzle with olive oil.

4 Bake on the oven's top shelf for 25–30 mins, without opening the oven, until golden. Transfer to a wire rack to cool before slicing.

Nutrition per serving (12)
energy 258 kcals, fat 10g, saturates 4g, carbs 32g, sugars 0g, fibre 1g, protein 10g, salt 0.7g

Pizza pie

Make a deep-dish Chicago-style pizza pie to serve everyone at once. This is a veggie version, but you can add any fillings you prefer.

 PREP 40 mins + proving/cooling COOK 50 mins   SERVES 6

FOR THE DOUGH
- 400g strong white bread flour, plus extra for dusting
- 7g sachet fast-action dried yeast
- pinch golden caster sugar
- 1 tsp salt
- 1 tbsp olive oil, plus extra for proving and the tin

FOR THE SAUCE
- 300ml passata
- 1 tbsp tomato purée
- 1 tbsp olive oil
- 1 garlic clove, finely grated
- 1 tsp dried oregano

FOR THE FILLING
- 2 large handfuls grated mozzarella (about 150g)
- 20 black olives, pitted and halved
- handful basil leaves

1 Mix the flour, yeast and sugar in a bowl, make a well and tip in salt, oil and 250ml tepid water. Bring into a dough with your hands. Knead on a floured surface for 10 mins until smooth and elastic. Put in an oiled bowl, cover with a damp tea towel and leave for 35–40 mins until doubled in size. Mix all the sauce ingredients.

2 Heat the oven to 190C/170C fan/gas 5. Oil a 23cm springform cake tin. Knock the air out of the dough a few times on a floured surface. Remove a quarter, then roll the rest out thinly enough to line the tin with some overhanging. Press into the base and up the sides of the tin.

3 Spread half the sauce over the base, then sprinkle with half the mozzarella, olives and basil. Roll the reserved dough out, then lay it over the top. Top with the remaining sauce, most of the cheese, the olives and basil. Fold the overhanging dough over slightly. Scatter the remaining cheese over the exposed filling.

4 Transfer to a baking tray. Bake for 45–50 mins until golden and crisp. Undo the clip and cool for 20 mins before removing from the tin.

Nutrition per serving
energy 390 kcals, fat 12g, saturates 5g, carbs 54g, sugars 3g, fibre 3g, protein 14g, salt 1.4g

Rye pizza with figs, fennel & gorgonzola

Give your pizza a gourmet makeover with top notch ingredients, including tangy Italian cheese and sweet ripe figs. Make sure the figs caramelise for a full flavour.

 PREP 1 hr + proving COOK 45 mins   MAKES 2 x 30cm pizzas

FOR THE DOUGH
- 5g dried yeast
- 250g strong white bread flour
- 125g '00' flour
- 125g rye flour
- 1 tsp salt
- ½ tsp sugar
- 1 tsp olive oil
- semolina flour, for dusting

FOR THE TOPPING
- 1 tbsp olive oil
- 2 onions, halved, finely sliced
- 1 large fennel bulb, quartered (fronds thinly sliced and tossed in the juice ½ small lemon)
- ¼ tsp fennel seeds, crushed
- extra virgin olive oil, for drizzling
- 12 small figs, halved
- 1½ tbsp balsamic vinegar
- caster sugar, for sprinkling
- 180g gorgonzola, crumbled
- 2 tbsp hazelnut halves, toasted

1 Mix the yeast, 2 tbsp warm water and 1 tbsp flour and leave until foamy. Using a stand mixer with a dough hook, mix the flours, yeast, salt, sugar, oil and 290ml warm water to a wet dough. Knead for 10 mins until smooth. Cover and leave to double in size for 2½–3 hrs.

2 Heat the olive oil and fry the onion and a pinch of salt for 7 mins. Add 2 tbsp water, cover and cook until softened. Add most of the fennel and the fennel seeds, season and cook for 3 mins, bubbling off any liquid.

3 Heat the oven to 220C/200 fan/gas 7 and put in a baking sheet to heat. Tip the dough onto a floured surface, squash down, then halve and roll, stretching into 2 thin 30–32cm circles.

4 Sprinkle 2 baking sheets with semolina and put the pizza bases on them. Top with the cooked onion, then raw fennel, extra virgin olive oil, halved figs, balsamic vinegar and a sprinkle of sugar and pepper. Cook each one on the heated baking sheet for 8–12 mins, adding the cheese halfway through. Finish with hazelnuts and fennel fronds.

Nutrition per serving
energy 698 kcals, fat 17g, saturates 6g, carbs 109g, sugars 46g, fibre 16g, protein 19g, salt 1.9g

Chapter 6

TEAR-&-SHARES

· ·

Tear-and-share breads are for pulling apart and eating with a group of friends. The dough is usually split into buns and left to rise close to each other, so once baked they are touching and easily rip off. You can flavour them with cheese, garlic butter or herbs. They can be baked around a Camembert for dunking or dipped into a spread or dip. These bakes are real showstoppers, lots of fun and are fantastic at a celebration or around the festive season.

Cheese & pesto whirls

These herby tear-and-share bread rolls have mozzarella and sun-dried tomatoes baked into them – perfect for a picnic or for dipping into soup.

 PREP 40 mins + cooling and rising COOK 40 mins   SERVES 12

- 450g strong white bread flour, plus extra for dusting
- 7g sachet fast-action dried yeast
- 1 tsp golden caster sugar
- 1½ tsp fine salt
- 2 tbsp olive oil, plus a drizzle
- 150g tub fresh pesto
- 240g tub semi-dried tomatoes, drained and roughly chopped
- 100g grated mozzarella (ready-grated is best for this, as it is drier than fresh)
- 50g Parmesan or vegetarian alternative, grated
- handful basil leaves

1 Put the flour, yeast, sugar and salt in the bowl of a stand mixer. Mix in 280ml warm water and the oil. Add 20ml more water if needed. Knead for 5 mins with the dough hook until soft and springy. Clean and oil the bowl, add the dough, cover and leave for about 1–3 hrs until double in size,

2 Line a baking tray with parchment. Punch the dough a couple of times with your fist, then tip onto a floured work surface. Dust the top and roll out to 40cm x 30cm. Spread the pesto over, then scatter over the tomatoes and cheeses. Roll up from one of the longer sides into a long sausage.

3 Cut the dough into 12. Place on the tray, cut-side up, seams on the inside, in a 3-by-4 formation, leaving a little space between each roll as they will grow. Loosely cover and leave for 30 mins–1 hr until almost doubled in size. Heat the oven to 200C/180C fan/gas 6.

4 Bake on the middle shelf for 35–40 mins until golden and the centre looks dry and not doughy. Cool for at least 10 mins.

Nutrition per serving
energy 293 kcals, fat 11g, saturates 3g, carbs 36g, sugars 8g, fibre 4g, protein 10g, salt 1.4g

Cheese, chive & ham tear-&-share

Bake this satisfying pull-apart loaf, stuffed with oozy cheese, mustard and ham. You can use any cheese you have in the fridge.

 PREP 45 mins + proving COOK 30 mins   MAKES 18 small rolls

- 170ml full-fat milk
- 1 tsp caster sugar
- 100g unsalted butter, cut into cubes
- 1½ tsp fine sea salt
- 3 tsp English mustard powder
- 500g strong white bread flour
- 7g sachet fast-action dried yeast
- 4 medium eggs, lightly beaten, plus 1 for glazing
- oil, for greasing
- 250g mature cheddar, grated
- 50g Parmesan, grated
- ½ bunch chives, finely chopped
- 150g smoked ham, coarsely chopped

1 Pour the milk into a pan and add the sugar and butter. Warm gently, swirling until the butter has melted. Set aside until lukewarm.

2 Mix the salt, mustard, flour and yeast in a bowl. Make a well, pour in the eggs and milk. Swiftly mix to a rough dough, then tip onto a floured surface and knead for 10–15 mins (7–10 mins in a stand mixer) until elastic and springy. Put in an oiled bowl in a warm place, cover with a tea towel and leave for 1½–2 hrs until doubled.

3 Knock the dough back on a floured surface by lightly punching and briefly kneading. Knead in half the cheese, all the chives and ham. Divide into 18 balls. Line a baking sheet with parchment and draw a 25cm round circle. Arrange the balls in concentric circles in the circle. Fill each gap with cheese. Cover lightly and leave for 1–1½ hrs until risen.

4 Heat the oven to 200C/180C fan/gas 6. Brush the dough with the glaze, sprinkle over most of the cheese, then bake for 25 mins. Sprinkle over the rest of the cheese and bake for 5 mins more. Cool a little before serving warm.

Nutrition per serving (2 rolls)
energy 505 kcals, fat 25g, saturates 14g, carbs 45g, sugars 2g, fibre 2g, protein 24g, salt 1.9g

Tear-&-share brioche with salmon pâté

Make our indulgent spring lunch, with golden, butter-laden tear-and-share brioche served with smoked salmon pâté. It's well worth the effort.

 PREP 1 hr + proving/chilling COOK 30 mins   SERVES 4-6

- 450g strong white bread flour, plus extra for dusting
- ½ small bunch chives, finely chopped
- 1½ tsp fine sea salt
- 30g caster sugar
- 7g sachet fast-action dried yeast
- 100ml full-fat milk, at hand-hot temperature
- 4 large eggs, room temperature, 3 beaten in a bowl, 1 in another
- 190g unsalted butter, cut into cubes and softened, plus extra for the bowl
- 400g smoked salmon pâté
- dill sprigs, to garnish

1 Put the flour in the bowl of a stand mixer with a dough hook. Add the chives and salt to one side of the bowl, and the sugar and yeast to the other. Mix each side into the flour, then slowly mix in the milk. Slowly add 3 eggs with the mixer on medium and mix for 10 mins. Add the butter, 1 or 2 cubes at a time, this will take another 5–8 mins. Cover and leave for 1½–2 hrs until doubled in size. Chill for 1 hr.

2 Line a large baking sheet with parchment. Tip the dough out onto a lightly floured work surface and divide into 18 balls. Butter the outside of a 12cm ovenproof bowl. Put it in the middle of the baking sheet and arrange the dough balls around it, leaving a 2cm space between each. Cover and leave for 30–35 mins until doubled in size.

3 Heat the oven to 180C/160C fan/gas 4. Brush the dough balls with beaten egg. Bake for 25–30 mins until golden and risen. Leave to cool for 20 mins, then lift the bowl out. Spoon the pâté into a small bowl, scatter over the dill and put in the middle to serve.

Nutrition per serving (6)
energy 748 kcals, fat 43g, saturates 24g, carbs 64g, sugars 7g, fibre 3g, protein 25g, salt 2.8g

Cheesy garlic bread

This goes with so many family dishes, such as chilli con carne, winter soups, salads and barbecues.

 PREP 20 mins + proving COOK 30 mins   MAKES 12 squares

- 500g strong white bread flour
- 7g sachet fast-action dried yeast
- 1 tsp salt
- 2 tbsp olive oil
- 1 tbsp clear honey
- 2 garlic cloves, crushed
- 25g soft butter
- 100g mature cheddar, grated
- handful thyme leaves

1 Measure the flour, yeast and salt into a large bowl. Mix 300ml hand-hot water with the oil and honey in a jug, then pour into the dry mix, stirring all the time to make a soft dough.

2 Turn the dough out onto a lightly floured surface, then knead for 5 mins until the dough no longer feels sticky, sprinkling with a little more flour as you need it. Now stretch it to fit a Swiss roll tin.

3 Mix the garlic with the butter, then dot over the dough. Sprinkle over the cheese and snip over the thyme. Cover the bread with lightly oiled cling film, then leave in a warm place to rise for 40 mins.

4 Heat the oven to 200C/fan 180C/gas 6. Remove the cling film, then bake the bread for 30 mins until golden and risen. Leave to cool for 10 mins, then cut into 12 pieces.

Nutrition per square
energy 215 kcals, fat 7g, saturates 3g, carbs 33g, sugars 2g, fibre 1g, protein 7g, salt 0.61g

Tear-&-share cheese & garlic rolls

Enjoy this cheesy garlic tear-and-share bread at a family dinner. It's perfect for feeding a crowd at a barbecue, or as a side dish to a hearty casserole.

 PREP 40 mins (plus at least 2 hrs proving) COOK 40 mins MAKES 20

- 100g unsalted butter, softened
- 450g strong white bread flour
- 7g sachet fast-action dried yeast
- 1 tsp golden caster sugar
- rapeseed oil, for the bowl and tray
- 2 tbsp polenta or cornmeal
- 1 garlic clove, grated
- 100g mozzarella, grated
- 50g cheddar, grated

1 Heat 280ml water with 50g butter until it melts, then cool to warm. Combine the flour, yeast, sugar and 1 tsp salt in a stand mixer. Add the water and mix to a soft dough then knead for 5 mins with dough hooks until the dough feels smooth and elastic. Cover and leave for 1½–2 hrs, or until doubled in size.

2 Brush a large baking tray with oil and scatter over the polenta. Squash down the dough with your fist. Pinch off pieces about the size of a walnut, roll each into a ball and put on the baking tray, spacing them out.

3 Heat oven to 180C/160C fan/gas 4. Cover the tray and leave for 30 mins–1 hr until doubled in size and the balls are touching. Mix the remaining butter with the garlic. Brush the tops with garlic butter and scatter with the cheeses. Bake for 25–30 mins until the dough balls are cooked through. Leave to cool for 5 mins, then serve.

Nutrition per serving
energy 150 kcals, fat 6g, saturates 4g, carbs 18g, sugars 0.3g, fibre 1g, protein 5g, salt 0.3g

Cheese-stuffed garlic dough balls

Impress family and friends with the ultimate sharing starter: cheesy, moreish garlic dough balls with a tomato dipping sauce. A great addition to an Italian dinner.

 PREP 40 mins + proving COOK 35 mins   MAKES 20-25

- 150g butter
- 300g strong white bread flour
- 7g sachet fast-action dried yeast
- 1 tbsp caster sugar
- 1 tsp salt
- 200g mozzarella, cut into 1.5cm cubes
- 65g Gruyère, grated (optional)
- 2 garlic cloves, crushed
- 1 rosemary sprig, leaves picked and finely chopped

FOR THE TOMATO SAUCE DIP

- 1 tbsp olive oil, plus extra for greasing
- 1 garlic clove, sliced
- 250g passata
- 1 tsp red wine vinegar
- 1 tsp caster sugar
- pinch chilli flakes
- ½ small bunch basil, torn, plus extra to serve

1 Heat 175ml water with 50g of the butter until it melts. Cool until warm. Combine the flour, yeast, sugar and salt in stand mixer. Add the water and mix to a soft dough, then knead with the dough hook for 10 mins until smooth. Cover and leave for 1½–2 hrs until doubled.

2 Line a baking sheet with parchment. Squash down the dough and knead for several minutes. Pinch off and flatten a small piece (about 20g) into a disc, put a mozzarella cube and pinch of Gruyère in the middle and fold in the sides to enclose, then roll into a ball. Put on the sheet. Repeat, spacing the balls ½cm apart. Cover and leave for 30 mins.

3 Melt the remaining butter and mix with the garlic and rosemary. Heat the oven to 180C/160C fan/gas 4. Brush the dough balls with the garlic butter and bake for 25–30 mins until golden and the middles are oozing.

4 Make the dip by frying the garlic in the oil for 30 seconds. Add the passata, vinegar, sugar and chilli. Simmer for 10 mins. Season and add the basil. Serve with the dough balls.

Nutrition per serving (25)
energy 123 kcals, fat 7g, saturates 4g, carbs 11g, sugars 1g, fibre 0g, protein 3g, salt 0.4g

Chapter 7

DAIRY- & GLUTEN-FREE BREADS

Even with a special diet, you need not miss out on homemade bread. You can make a classic loaf wheat or dairy-free with these tried-and-tested recipes. The method may differ slightly, but the final result will be equally as tasty. From gluten-free pizza to vegan hot cross buns, this chapter covers a range of breads for those who struggle with intolerances or follow a special diet.

Gluten-free bread

A straightforward loaf of bread for anyone who's following a gluten-free diet. Bake this and use it to make sandwiches or toast, or simply slather it in butter.

 PREP 5 mins + proving COOK 1 hr    MAKES 1 loaf (cuts into 10–12 slices)

- 400g gluten-free white flour
- 1 tsp salt
- 7g sachet fast-action dried yeast
- 284ml pot buttermilk (or the same amount of whole milk with a squeeze of lemon juice)
- 2 eggs
- 2 tbsp olive oil, plus extra for greasing

1 Heat the oven to 180C/160C fan/gas 4. Mix the flour, salt and yeast in a large bowl. In a separate bowl, whisk together the buttermilk, eggs and oil. Mix the wet ingredients into the dry to make a sticky dough.

2 Grease a 900g loaf tin, or flour a baking sheet. With oiled hands, shape the dough into a sausage shape for a loaf or a ball for a cob. If making a loaf, place the dough in the tin. For a cob, place it on the baking sheet and score the top with a sharp knife. Cover loosely with a piece of oiled cling film and leave somewhere warm for 1 hr until risen by a third or so.

3 Bake for 50–60 mins until golden and well risen. Turn out onto a wire rack and leave to cool for at least 20 mins before cutting.

Nutrition per serving (12)
energy 136 kcals, fat 3g, saturates 1g, carbs 23g, sugars 1g, fibre 0.5g, protein 4g, salt 0.52g

Gluten-free chilli cornbread

Golden polenta and frozen sweetcorn make a deliciously different alternative to your regular loaf – best eaten fresh from the oven.

 PREP 20 mins + soaking COOK 30 mins   SERVES 4–6

- 200g polenta or fine ground cornmeal
- 284ml pot buttermilk
- 25g butter
- 1 red chilli, deseeded and finely chopped
- 1 tsp gluten-free baking powder
- ¼ tsp bicarbonate of soda
- 50g frozen sweetcorn, defrosted
- 2 large eggs, beaten
- ½ tsp salt

1 Lightly toast the polenta in a dry frying pan for 3–4 mins, stirring to ensure even cooking, until the polenta has heated through, is fragrant and small patches are starting to turn golden brown. Take off the heat, tip half into a large bowl and add the buttermilk. Stir well, cover and leave to soak for 2–3 hrs.

2 Melt the butter in a 25cm ovenproof frying pan (a cast-iron one is perfect) and heat the oven to 220C/200C fan/gas 7. Stir the butter and the remaining ingredients, including the rest of the toasted polenta, into the buttermilk and polenta mixture. (Don't wipe out the frying pan – the slick of butter will ensure the bread doesn't stick.)

3 Put the pan back on the heat and turn up the temperature. Pour the mixture into the pan – it should sizzle as it hits it, like a Yorkshire pudding. Put the whole pan in the oven and bake for 15–20 mins until golden brown and firm in the middle. Leave to cool a little, then serve cut into wedges.

Nutrition per serving (6)
energy 200 kcals, fat 6g, saturates 3g, carbs 29g, sugars 3g, fibre 1g, protein 7g, salt 1g

Vegan banana & walnut bread

We love a slice of banana bread with crunchy walnuts and sweet dates, warm from the oven. This vegan version is great for breakfast or with an afternoon cuppa.

 PREP 20 mins COOK 1 hr SERVES 8

- 200g self-raising flour
- 25g ground almonds
- 1 tsp baking powder
- 75g light muscovado sugar
- 4 dates, finely chopped
- 3–4 very ripe bananas, mashed
- 50ml coconut oil or sunflower oil, plus extra greasing
- 3 tbsp soya milk
- 75g walnut pieces, toasted

1 Heat the oven to 200C/180C fan/gas 6. Brush a 450g loaf tin with a little oil then line with parchment.

2 Mix the flour, almonds, baking powder, sugar and dates. Beat together the mashed banana and oil, then combine it with the flour mixture. Add the soya milk to loosen the mixture, fold in the walnuts and scrape the mixture into the tin. Bake for 1 hr, covering the top if it starts to look too brown. Insert a skewer into the centre of the bread – it should come out clean. If not, return to the oven and cook for a further 10 mins. Cool for 15 mins before taking it out of the tin.

Nutrition per serving
energy 315 kcals, fat 15g, saturates 6g, carbs 38g, sugars 18g, fibre 2g, protein 6g, salt 0.3g

Gluten-free sundried tomato bread

A quick, gluten-free bread recipe with cheese and tomatoes – no need for yeast, this loaf is ready in under an hour.

 PREP 15 mins COOK 1 hr   MAKES 1 loaf

- 200g gluten-free white flour
- 1 tsp salt
- 3 tsp gluten-free baking powder
- 284ml pot buttermilk (or the same amount of whole milk with a squeeze of lemon juice)
- 3 eggs
- 1 tsp tomato purée
- 2 tbsp olive oil
- 50g sundried tomatoes in oil (about 6–8), coarsely chopped
- 25g Parmesan or vegetarian alternative, grated

1 Heat the oven to 180C/fan 160C/gas 4. Mix the flour, salt and baking powder in a large bowl. In a separate bowl, whisk together the buttermilk, eggs, tomato purée and oil. Fold the wet ingredients into the dry, then add the sundried tomatoes and half the Parmesan.

2 Grease a 900g loaf tin and pour in the mixture. Sprinkle the remaining Parmesan on top and bake for 50–60 mins until a skewer inserted into the middle comes out clean. Turn out onto a wire rack to cool.

Nutrition per serving
energy 74 kcals, fat 3g, saturates 1g, carbs 10g, sugars 0g, fibre 1g, protein 3g, salt 0.7g

Gluten-free pizza

Make our gluten-free version of a classic pizza. The base is easy to make, then spread over rich homemade tomato sauce and finish with buffalo mozzarella and fresh basil.

 PREP 45 mins COOK 10 mins   SERVES 4

FOR THE GLUTEN-FREE BASE
- 400g gluten-free bread flour
- 2 heaped tsp golden caster sugar
- 2 tsp gluten-free baking powder
- 1 tsp fine salt
- 1 heaped tsp xanthan gum
- 5 tbsp olive oil

FOR THE SAUCE & TOPPING
- 2 tbsp olive oil
- 1 small onion, finely chopped
- 1 x 400g can chopped tomatoes
- 2 tbsp tomato purée
- 1 tsp caster sugar
- ½ small bunch basil, leaves shredded
- 2 x 125g balls buffalo mozzarella

1 Mix the flour, sugar, baking powder, salt and xanthan gum in a bowl. Stir in 250ml warm water and the olive oil. Combine quickly with your hands to a thick, wet, paste, adding an extra 20ml warm water if the dough feels dry. Store, covered, in the fridge for up to 24 hours.

2 Make the sauce: heat the oil and fry the onion with a pinch of salt over a low heat until softened, about 10 mins. Add the tomatoes, purée and sugar and simmer for 25–30 mins until thick. Blitz with a blender, season and stir through the basil. Cool.

3 Heat the oven to 220C/200 fan/gas 7 and put 2 baking sheets inside. Lightly flour 2 more baking sheets. Split the dough into 2 and flatten half onto each sheet with your fingers to make 2 x 20–25cm bases.

4 Finish the bases with a thin layer of the sauce and torn up mozzarella. Place the baking sheets on top of the hot baking sheets in the oven and cook for 8–10 mins or until crisp around the edges.

Nutrition per serving
energy 740 kcals, fat 33g, saturates 12g, carbs 90g, sugars 9g, fibre 4g, protein 18g, salt 2.54g

Vegan hot cross buns

What says Easter better than hot cross buns? Try this vegan version, with cinnamon, spice, sultanas and citrus bringing the traditional flavours.

 PREP 35 mins + proving COOK 20 mins   MAKES 12

- 300ml unsweetened almond milk
- 50g dairy-free spread
- 500g strong white bread flour
- 7g sachet fast-action dried yeast
- 70g golden caster sugar
- ½ tsp salt
- 2 heaped tsp ground cinnamon
- 2 heaped tsp mixed spice
- 1 large orange, zested
- 70g sultanas
- 50g mixed peel

FOR THE CROSSES & GLAZE

- 70g plain flour
- 50g apricot jam

YOU WILL NEED

- piping bag with a small round nozzle

1 Put the milk in a pan and, once simmering, add the spread. Remove from the heat and allow to melt, then cool to hand temperature.

2 Mix the flour, yeast, sugar, salt and spices in a bowl. Make a well and pour in the milk, swiftly mixing to a sticky dough. Tip onto a floured surface. Knead by stretching back and forth for 5–7 mins until smooth, springy and elastic. Shape into a ball, put in an oiled bowl, cover and leave in a warm spot for 1hr until doubled.

3 Tip the dough back onto the surface; flatten into a round. Spread on the zest, sultanas and peel and knead in. Form into a ball, return to the bowl, cover and leave for 1hr.

4 Line a baking sheet. Knock the dough back by gently punching out the air. Roll into 12 balls and place on the sheet, leaving space. Cover with oiled cling film and leave for 45 mins.

5 Heat the oven to 220C/ 200 fan/ gas 7. Mix the flour with 1 tbsp water at a time to create a thick paste and use the piping bag to pipe crosses. Bake for 15–20 mins, then heat the jam and brush over the buns.

Nutrition per serving
energy 268 kcals, fat 3g, saturates 1g, carbs 51g, sugars 15g, fibre 3g, protein 6g, salt 0.34g

Gluten-free banana bread

Use up overripe bananas and make banana bread with ground almonds and gluten-free flour. This recipe is ideal for anyone following a gluten-free diet.

 PREP 10 mins COOK 1¼ hrs SERVES 8

- 5 small ripe bananas, 4 mashed, 1 sliced down the middle to decorate the top
- 150g gluten-free self-raising flour
- 100g gluten-free oats
- 50g ground almonds
- 1 tsp gluten-free baking powder
- 1 tsp ground cinnamon
- 90g dark brown sugar
- 90g caster sugar
- 100g butter, melted
- 2 large eggs, beaten
- 1 tbsp icing sugar

1 Heat the oven to 180C/160C fan/gas 4 and line a 900g loaf tin with parchment (our tin was 19cm x 9cm x 6cm). Put all the ingredients except the sliced banana, 1 tbsp caster sugar and the icing sugar into a large bowl and stir until smooth and combined.

2 Pour into the tin and put the 2 remaining banana halves, cut-side up, across the top of the batter, pressing down slightly. Sprinkle over the caster sugar. Bake for 1–1¼ hrs until a skewer comes out clean, covering with foil towards the end of the cooking time if it browns too much.

3 Dust with icing sugar and leave to cool.

Nutrition per serving
energy 405 kcals, fat 16g, saturates 7g, carbs 57g, sugars 33g, fibre 2g, protein 7g, salt 0.6g

Vegan pizza Margherita

Vegans needn't miss out on pizza Margherita. Our recipe combines the classic flavours of this Italian comfort food using plant-based substitutes.

 PREP 15 mins + proving COOK 15 mins   SERVES 4 (makes 2 large or 4 small pizzas)

FOR THE PIZZA DOUGH
- 500g strong white bread flour, plus extra for dusting
- 1 tsp dried yeast
- 1 tsp caster sugar
- 1½ tbsp olive oil, plus extra for greasing and drizzling
- 1 tsp salt

FOR THE TOMATO SAUCE
- 100ml passata
- 1 tbsp fresh basil, chopped (or ½ tsp dried oregano)
- 1 garlic clove, crushed
- pinch sugar (optional)

FOR THE TOPPING
- 2 tomatoes, thinly sliced
- 200g vegan mozzarella-style cheese, grated
- basil or oregano leaves, chilli oil and vegan parmesan, to serve (optional)

1 Put the flour, yeast and sugar in a bowl. Stir in 300ml warm water, the oil and salt. Knead in the bowl until it forms a soft, slightly sticky dough. If it's dry, add a splash of cold water.

2 Knead on a floured work surface for 10 mins. Leave in the bowl, covered with oiled cling film, in a warm place for 1 hr until doubled.

3 Heat the oven to 220C/200C/gas 9 and put a baking sheet or pizza stone on the top shelf. Knock the dough back by punching a couple of times with your fist, then kneading. It should be springy and less sticky. Mix the ingredients for the tomato sauce together and season.

4 Divide the dough into 2 or 4 balls and flatten out as thin as you can get them, flouring to stop them sticking. Flour another baking sheet and put a pizza base on top. Spread over 4–5 tbsp tomato sauce, the tomato slices and cheese. Drizzle with olive oil and bake on top of your heated baking tray for 10–12 mins.

5 Repeat with the rest of the dough and toppings. Serve with herbs, chilli oil if you like and sprinkle over parmesan just after baking.

Nutrition per serving
energy 688 kcals, fat 20g, saturates 11g, carbs 107g, sugars 4g, fibre 5g, protein 18g, salt 2g

Chapter 8

RECIPES USING BREAD

Bread can often turn stale quickly and therefore is no longer best for eating as it is. This collection of recipes showcases ways to transform your leftover loaf into a new and exciting dish. Revamp it by baking slices into a custardy dessert or turning it into French toast. This chapter also shows you how to use your bread in other recipes. From fantastic baguette fillings to new ways with toasties, we've got you covered.

Ricotta strawberry French toast

Give your French toast a summer makeover with fresh berries, lashings of ricotta, honey and mint.

 PREP 10 mins COOK 20 mins  SERVES 2

- 1 large egg, beaten
- 300ml milk
- 1 tsp vanilla extract
- 4 slices thick-cut white bread
- 2 tbsp butter
- 50g ricotta
- 2 tbsp honey
- 100g strawberries, some sliced, some halved
- 2 mint sprigs, leaves picked

1 In a wide dish, whisk the egg, milk and vanilla together. Coat one side of the bread slices in the liquid, then carefully flip them over and leave them to soak for 1–2 mins.

2 Melt 1 tbsp of the butter in a large non-stick pan over a medium heat and add 2 slices of bread. Cook for 5 mins or until golden, then turn to cook the other side for another 5 mins. Transfer to a plate and cook the other 2 slices in the rest of the butter.

3 Halve the toast on the diagonal and spread each slice with the ricotta. Drizzle over the honey and a pinch of flaky sea salt, and arrange some sliced strawberries in a fan across the toast. Decorate the plate with the halved strawberries and mint.

Nutrition per serving
energy 540 kcals, fat 21g, saturates 12g, carbs 64g, sugars 29g, fibre 4g, protein 19g, salt 1.5g

Blueberry bostock

Say hello to your new favourite breakfast! A cross between French toast and an almond croissant, we've used blueberries, but you can top it with any fruit.

 PREP 15 mins + cooling COOK 30 mins SERVES 6

- 3 tbsp caster sugar
- 1 strip pared lemon zest
- 6 slices day-old brioche or thickly sliced white sandwich loaf (roughly 10cm x 10cm slices)
- 100g blueberries
- 50g flaked almonds
- crème fraîche, to serve (optional)

FOR THE FRANGIPANE
- 100g butter, softened
- 100g caster sugar
- 75g ground almonds
- 1 tbsp plain flour
- ¼ tsp almond extract
- 1 egg

1 Heat the oven to 180C/160C fan/gas 4 and line a baking tray with parchment. Put the caster sugar and 3 tbsp water in a small saucepan, and add the lemon zest. Bring to a simmer, bubble for a minute until the sugar has dissolved, then set aside to cool a little.

2 To make the frangipane, beat the butter and sugar together for a few minutes with an electric whisk. Add the ground almonds, flour, almond extract and egg, and beat for another minute until well combined.

3 Lay the slices of bread on the tray, then brush the syrup over until it's used up. Divide the frangipane among the slices of brioche and spread right to the edges. Put a handful of blueberries in the centre of each piece, then press as many flaked almonds around the edge of each piece as you can make stick.

4 Bake for 25–30 mins until the frangipane is golden brown. Cool for at least 10 mins before eating, then serve with a spoonful of crème fraîche, if you like.

Nutrition per serving
energy 637 kcals, fat 35g, saturates 16g, carbs 67g, sugars 37g, fibre 2g, protein 12g, salt 0.9g

Bread-&-butter pudding

Transform a stale loaf into a comforting bread-and-butter pudding. This traditional British dessert is layered with a rich vanilla custard, dried fruit and lemon zest.

 PREP 20 mins COOK 45 mins   SERVES 6

- 250ml full-fat milk
- 300ml double cream
- 1 vanilla pod, halved and seeds scraped out or 1 tsp vanilla extract
- 3 large eggs, plus 1 egg yolk
- 3 tbsp golden caster sugar
- 8 slices day-old white crusty bread
- 50g slightly salted butter, softened, plus extra for greasing
- 75g mix sultanas and currants or other dried fruit
- zest ½ lemon
- 2 tbsp demerara sugar

1 Heat the oven to 180C/160C/gas 4. To make the custard, heat the milk, cream and vanilla pod with its scraped-out seeds (if using) in a pan to just below boiling point. Whisk the eggs and yolk with the caster sugar in a jug. Slowly pour the warm milk mixture, including the pod, over the eggs, stirring constantly until smooth. Stir in the vanilla extract now if using.

2 Lightly butter a roughly 20cm x 25cm x 5cm ovenproof dish. Cut the crusts from the bread slices, then butter both sides of the bread and cut into triangles. Lay half of the bread slices in the bottom of the dish so that they are slightly overlapping. Mix the dried fruit with the lemon zest and sprinkle half of the mix over the bread. Layer the rest of the bread on top then sprinkle over the remaining fruit.

3 Remove the vanilla pod from the custard then pour over the pudding. Leave to soak for at least 30 mins, or longer in the fridge, if you like. Sprinkle over the demerara and bake for 35–40 mins until golden brown and puffed up.

Nutrition per serving
energy 566 kcals, fat 40g, saturates 23g, carbs 42g, sugars 29g, fibre 1g, protein 9g, salt 0g

Rhubarb ricotta bread-&-butter pudding

This indulgent spring bread-and-butter pudding is full of seasonal rhubarb and rich ricotta, perfect for entertaining a crowd with a sweet tooth.

 PREP 25 mins + resting COOK 50 mins   SERVES 8

- 150g golden caster sugar
- 400g rhubarb, trimmed and cut into 3cm pieces
- 300ml full-fat milk
- 300ml double cream
- ½ tsp vanilla extract
- 3 large eggs, plus 1 egg yolk
- 200g ricotta
- 25g icing sugar, plus extra for dusting
- about 250g bread (soft white rolls, sliced bread or brioche)
- 35g butter
- 1 lemon, zested
- 1 orange, zested
- crème fraîche or cream and Greek yogurt, to serve

1 Heat 100ml water in a pan with 50g of the sugar. Bring to the boil and add the rhubarb. Simmer for 1½ mins, then lift the rhubarb out with a slotted spoon. Arrange it on a plate or tray so that it can lie in a single layer.

2 Put the milk, cream and a pinch of salt in a heavy-bottomed pan and bring to the boil, then add the vanilla. Beat the eggs, yolk and rest of the sugar together in a bowl. Pour the warm milk and cream onto this, stirring all the time. Heat the oven to 180C/160C fan/gas 4.

3 Drain the ricotta, then add the icing sugar. Butter the bread and spread with ricotta. Sprinkle the citrus zest on top, then layer with the rhubarb in a 20cm x 30cm ovenproof dish. Pour the egg and cream mixture through a sieve and leave for 30 mins.

4 Put the dish in a roasting tin. Add enough boiling water to the tin to come halfway up the sides of the dish. Bake for 40–45 mins or until puffy, set and golden. Cool for 10 mins. Dust with icing sugar and serve with crème fraîche or cream mixed with Greek yogurt.

Nutrition per serving
energy 489 kcals, fat 32g, saturates 18g, carbs 39g, sugars 26g, fibre 2g, protein 11g, salt 0.7g

Egg-in-the-hole bacon sandwich

Who says fillings have to be on the inside? An old favourite is given a modern twist in this egg and bacon sandwich as the egg is served within the bread.

 PREP 5 mins COOK 15 mins   SERVES 1

- oil, for frying
- 4 rashers smoked streaky bacon
- 2 thick slices sourdough
- 1 tbsp mayonnaise
- 1 small egg
- 1 tbsp ketchup or brown sauce, to serve

1 Heat a splash of oil in a large, non-stick frying pan. Fry the bacon until crispy, then put on a plate covered with foil to keep warm.

2 Using a cookie cutter, cut a hole in 1 slice of bread, then spread mayonnaise on one side of both slices. Fry the bread in the same pan. When brown on one side, flip both over and crack the egg into the hole. Fry for 2–3 mins, then turn down the heat and cover the pan until the white of the egg is set but the yolk is still runny. Remove everything from the pan.

3 Spread the non-egg slice with the sauce, add the bacon, then top with the egg slice. Halve and tuck in.

Nutrition per serving
energy 802 kcals, fat 57g, saturates 11g, carbs 36g, sugars 3g, fibre 2g, protein 36g, salt 4.8g

Christmas leftover sandwich

Take your Boxing Day sarnie to the next level. Hollow out a loaf of bread and layer up all your Christmas leftovers inside it to make a lip-smacking sandwich.

 PREP 15 mins + chilling SERVES 4-6

- 400g white round crusty loaf
- 2 tbsp mayonnaise
- 2 tsp English mustard
- 3–4 tbsp cranberry sauce
- handful baby spinach
- 3–4 tbsp crispy onions
- 250g leftover roast turkey
- 6 leftover cooked pigs in blankets, halved lengthways
- 150g leftover cooked stuffing

1 Slice a roughly 3cm lid off the top of the loaf. Scoop out most of the bread from the loaf and lid, leaving about a 1cm layer (you can use the scooped-out bread for croutons or in another recipe).

2 Combine the mayonnaise and mustard, then spread 2 tbsp over the inside of the loaf, and 1 tbsp inside the lid. Spoon most of the cranberry sauce into the lid, followed by half the spinach, the crispy onions, and half the turkey. Arrange the rest of the turkey in the base of the loaf, followed by the rest of the cranberry sauce, the pigs in blankets, stuffing and remaining spinach. Top the loaf with the stuffed lid, press down lightly, then tightly wrap and chill for at least 3 hrs. Slice into 4 or 6 wedges to serve.

Nutrition per serving (6)
energy 504 kcals, fat 25g, saturates 5g, carbs 42g, sugars 7g, fibre 2g, protein 27g, salt 1.8g

Chorizo & halloumi breakfast baguette

Treat yourself to this hearty baguette – perfect for the weekend. Make the tomato jam in advance and then enjoy it on sausage sarnies, a cheeseboard or with chicken.

 PREP 15 mins + cooling COOK 40 mins   SERVES 4

- 1 large avocado
- 1 lime, juiced
- 1 red onion, thinly sliced
- drizzle oil
- 150g chorizo, sliced
- 250g halloumi, sliced into 8
- 1 large baguette or 2 smaller ones
- small bunch coriander, leaves picked

FOR THE TOMATO JAM
- 400g can chopped tomatoes
- red chilli, finely chopped (deseeded if you don't want much spice)
- thumb-sized piece ginger, grated
- 1 star anise
- 250g caster sugar
- 150ml red wine vinegar

1 To make the tomato jam, put all the ingredients in a pan, season and simmer for 30 mins until you have a rich, thick glossy jam. Cool, then transfer to a sterilised jar (if you want to keep for over 2 weeks). Will keep, unopened, for 6 months.

2 Halve the avocado and scoop into a bowl. Add half the lime juice and some salt and mash with a fork. Put the onion in a small bowl, pour over the rest of the lime juice and season with a pinch of salt. Mix well and set aside to lightly pickle.

3 Heat a drizzle of oil in a large frying pan. Cook the chorizo slices on one side of the pan and the halloumi on the other, turning once the halloumi is golden and the chorizo is sizzling. Cook for about 4–5 mins in total.

4 Meanwhile, split and warm the baguette in the oven. Spread the avocado over one side of the baguette, and the tomato jam over the other. Fill with the halloumi, chorizo, coriander and pickled red onions. Cut up and tuck in.

Nutrition per serving
energy 872 kcals, fat 39g, saturates 17g, carbs 91g, sugars 38g, fibre 7g, protein 36g, salt 4.2g

Fig, burrata & prosciutto tartine

Use larger slices of sourdough for our fig, burrata and prosciutto tartines for an impressive-looking lunch or starter that's deceptively easy.

 PREP 5 mins COOK 5 mins   SERVES 4

- 4 slices sourdough
- olive oil, for drizzling
- 2 tbsp fig chutney
- 2 x 100g balls burrata, drained
- 8 slices prosciutto
- 4–6 ripe figs, roughly torn or halved
- handful thyme or oregano, leaves picked
- balsamic vinegar, to serve

1 Heat a griddle pan over a high heat or heat the grill to high. Drizzle each side of the bread with a little olive oil, then toast in the pan or under the grill for 2 mins on each side until golden brown.

2 Spread the fig chutney over the toasted bread. Tear or chop the burrata into chunky pieces and arrange these on the toast, create little nests of prosciutto on top, then add the fig pieces. Sprinkle with the thyme, then drizzle with more olive oil and a little balsamic vinegar.

Nutrition per serving
energy 519 kcals, fat 19g, saturates 9g, carbs 64g, sugars 31g, fibre 7g, protein 19g, salt 2.3g

Mango chutney & cheese naan toastie

A reinvented veggie cheese toastie, using sweet mango chutney, mozzarella, cheddar and garlic naan bread. A must-try lunch or dinner for cheese fans.

 PREP 10 mins COOK 10 mins   SERVES 1

- 50g mature cheddar, grated
- 50g hard mozzarella, grated
- 3 spring onions, thinly sliced
- 1 small green chilli, finely chopped
- ½ tsp cumin seeds
- 1 tbsp coriander, roughly chopped
- 1 large round garlic naan bread
- 1 tbsp mango chutney, plus extra to serve
- 10g butter

1 In a bowl, mix the cheeses, spring onion, chilli, cumin seeds and coriander.

2 Cut the naan in half down the centre. Spread one half with the chutney, top with the cheese mixture, then cover with the other half. Melt the butter in a frying pan over a medium heat until just beginning to foam. Add the naan sandwich and use something heavy like a saucepan to press it down. Fry on one side for 4–5 mins or until golden brown, then turn over and repeat. Both sides should be crisp, with the cheese gooey. Cut in half and serve with extra chutney.

Nutrition per serving
energy 869 kcals, fat 47g, saturates 24g, carbs 75g, sugars 12g, fibre 4g, protein 35g, salt 3.1g

Meatball & garlic bread traybake

Make this comforting meatball and garlic bread traybake for a dinner the whole family will enjoy. You could buy a pack of meatballs if you're short on time.

 PREP 10 mins COOK 50 mins SERVES 3 (or 2 adults and 2 children)

- 350g turkey thigh mince
- 1 tsp dried oregano
- 1 tsp fennel seeds
- 1½ tbsp olive oil
- 1 large onion, chopped
- 3 garlic cloves, crushed
- 1 tbsp tomato purée
- 2 x 400g cans chopped tomatoes
- 2 tsp sugar
- 150g ball mozzarella, torn into pieces
- 4 garlic bread slices or garlic breadsticks, torn or chopped into chunks
- 25g cheddar, grated
- green salad or spaghetti, to serve

1 Combine the mince, oregano, fennel seeds and some seasoning in a bowl. Take walnut-sized pieces of the mixture and roll into balls. Heat half the oil in a large, shallow ovenproof pan and cook the meatballs until browned all over – don't worry if they're not cooked through. Transfer to a plate. Heat the oven to 200C/180C fan/gas 6.

2 Heat the remaining oil in the pan and add the onion. Cook until softened, about 10–12 mins, stirring regularly. Stir in the garlic for another minute, then the tomato purée, chopped tomatoes and sugar.

3 Simmer for 10–15 mins, then season to taste. Place the meatballs on top of the sauce, then add the mozzarella, garlic bread and the cheddar on top. Bake for 15–20 mins until golden and crisp.

Nutrition per serving
energy 565 kcals, fat 28g, saturates 13g, carbs 34g, sugars 19g, fibre 6g, protein 42g, salt 1.3g

Eggy bread

The simplest of indulgent breakfast recipes. Serve our eggy bread by itself, with an oozy fruit compote or as part of a traditional fried breakfast.

 PREP 5 mins COOK 5 mins  SERVES 1

- 2 medium eggs
- 1 tbsp milk
- 2 slices white or brown bread
- 1 tbsp butter
- crispy bacon or fruit compote, to serve

1 Lightly beat the eggs in a shallow bowl along with the milk. Season with salt and black pepper.

2 Dip each slice of bread into the egg mixture, making sure it has soaked up all of the liquid. Heat a frying pan over a medium heat and add the butter. Swirl the butter around the pan and when it's beginning to foam, add the bread and fry on each side for 1 min or until golden brown. Transfer to a plate and serve with crispy bacon or fruit compote.

Nutrition per serving
energy 376 kcals, fat 23g, saturates 11g, carbs 23g, sugars 2g, fibre 1g, protein 19g, salt 1.21g

Spiced prawn cocktail subs

Forget boring sandwiches at a picnic – pack these prawn cocktail subs instead. If you're travelling, assemble them when you get there so they're super-fresh.

 PREP 10 mins   MAKES 6 small rolls

- 3 tbsp mayonnaise
- 1 tbsp mango chutney
- ¼ tsp mild curry powder
- squeeze lemon or lime juice
- 150g cooked North Atlantic prawns
- 6 small sub rolls
- 1 small Little Gem lettuce, leaves picked
- small chunk cucumber, thinly sliced

1 Mix the mayonnaise, mango chutney and curry powder with a squeeze of lemon or lime juice in a bowl. Stir in the prawns, then chill until you're ready to assemble.

2 To serve, split the sub rolls across the top, line each one with a lettuce leaf and a few slices of cucumber, then spoon in the prawn filling.

Nutrition per serving
energy 199 kcals, fat 7g, saturates 1g, carbs 24g, sugars 3g, fibre 2g, protein 9g, salt 0.9g

Chapter 9

SWEET BREADS

· ·

Sweet breads are enriched with sugar or honey and often butter to make the crumb richer and more indulgent. From classic doughnuts to cinnamon rolls, a sweet bread is a great alternative to baking a cake or batch of biscuits.

Twisted bread with honey tahini butter

You can serve this warm or leave it to cool, it's best eaten on the day you make it. To make things extra indulgent, spread thick slices with our honey and tahini butter.

 PREP 35 mins + proving COOK 40 mins   SERVES 10–12

- 120–140ml whole milk
- 50g unsalted butter, cubed
- 300g strong white bread flour, plus extra for dusting
- 50g golden caster sugar
- ½ tsp fine sea salt
- 7g sachet fast-action dried yeast
- 1 medium egg, lightly beaten
- 75g golden icing sugar
- sesame seeds (optional)

FOR THE FILLING
- 50g unsalted butter, softened
- 2 tbsp sesame seeds, toasted
- 50g light brown soft sugar
- 3 tsp ground cinnamon
- ¼ tsp ground cardamom

FOR THE HONEY TAHINI BUTTER
- 70g salted butter, softened
- 2 tbsp runny honey
- 2 tbsp tahini

1 Warm 120ml milk and the butter until melted. Cool to lukewarm. Combine the flour, sugar, salt and yeast in a stand mixer. Mix in the egg and milk, adding more milk if dry. Knead with the dough hook for 5–8 mins until smooth. Leave, covered, for 1–1½ hrs until doubled.

2 To make the filling, combine the ingredients and set aside. To make the tahini butter, mix the ingredients with a pinch of salt.

3 Line a large baking sheet. Roll the dough out on a lightly floured surface to a 40cm square. Spread the filling evenly over the dough, leaving a 2cm border. Roll the dough towards you into a tight log, lift onto the baking sheet. Cut the log in half lengthways down the middle and open, cut-side up. Pinch together at one end, then twist together like a rope. Cover and leave for 45 mins–1 hr to rise.

4 Heat the oven to 180C/160C fan/gas 4. Bake for 35–40 mins until golden and hollow sounding when tapped on the base. Cool briefly. Mix the icing sugar with 1 tbsp water, drizzle over and sprinkle with sesame seeds.

Nutrition per serving (12)
energy 304 kcals, fat 15g, saturates 8g, carbs 36g, sugars 18g, fibre 2g, protein 5g, salt 0.4g

Raspberry, chocolate & hazelnut bread

This brunch loaf requires good kneading skills – prepare the dough ahead and then pop it in the oven to serve warm with butter, jam and more chocolate hazelnut spread.

 PREP 1 hour + up to 3 days chilling COOK 40 mins   SERVES 8–10

- 2 x 7g sachets fast-action dried yeast
- 600g '00' flour, sponge flour or plain flour, plus extra for dusting
- 50g golden caster sugar
- 1 tsp salt
- 400ml warm milk
- 50g melted salted butter, plus extra for greasing
- 1 large egg, beaten
- 200g chocolate hazelnut spread
- 200g raspberries
- 1–2 tbsp chopped hazelnuts
- 1 tbsp granulated sugar

1 Up to 3 days before baking (at least 1 day), mix the yeast, 400g of the flour, sugar and salt in a bowl. Whisk the milk, butter and egg and stir into the flour. Cover tightly with oiled cling film and chill overnight or for up to 3 days.

2 When you're ready to bake, heat the oven to 180C/160C fan/gas 4. Add the remaining flour to the dough and use your hands to mix in. Tip onto a floured surface and lightly knead together. Roll out with more flour to a 50cm x 30cm rectangle. Spread the chocolate over the dough, scatter over the raspberries, then press lightly so they stick into the dough.

3 With a long side facing you, roll up as tightly as you can (like a Swiss roll). Use a sharp knife, dusted with a little flour, to cut in half down the length – but not quite through at one end so the 2 strips are still joined. Twist the 2 strips together, then bring the ends together to make a wreath, pinching to stick. Lift onto a baking sheet, scatter with the hazelnuts and sugar, and bake for 30–40 mins until browned and crusty. Cool until just warm.

Nutrition per serving (10)
energy 422 kcals, fat 14g, saturates 6g, carbs 64g, sugars 22g, fibre 4g, protein 10g, salt 0.7g

Doughnuts

To fill these sugary treats, make a hole with a small knife in the side of each and pipe in the filling. Try custard, lemon curd or jam.

 PREP 45 mins + proving/overnight chilling COOK 40 mins (4 mins each)   MAKES 20

- 500g strong white bread flour
- 60g golden caster sugar, plus extra for tossing
- 15g fresh yeast, crumbled
- 4 eggs
- zest ½ lemon
- 2 tsp fine sea salt
- 125g unsalted butter, softened, cut into 25g pieces
- about 2 litres sunflower oil, for deep-frying

1 Put 150g water and all the ingredients, except the butter, into the bowl of a stand mixer with a beater paddle. Mix on medium for 8 mins or until the dough starts to form a ball. Let the dough rest for 1 min, then slowly add the butter on medium. Finally, mix on high for 5 mins until the dough is glossy and very elastic. Cover and leave until doubled in size. Squash down, then re-cover and chill overnight.

2 The next day, cut the dough into 20 pieces. Roll into smooth, tight buns and put on a floured baking tray, spacing well apart. Cover and leave for 4 hrs until doubled in size.

3 Fill your deep-fat fryer or heavy-based pan halfway with oil. Heat the oil to 180C.

4 Carefully slide the doughnuts in, 2 or 3 at a time, without deflating them. Fry for 2 mins each side until golden. They float, so you may need to gently push them down. Keep checking the oil temperature to keep it constant. Lift out and drain on kitchen paper. Toss in a bowl of caster sugar while still warm.

Nutrition per doughnut
energy 225 kcals, fat 16g, saturates 4g, carbs 22g, sugars 3g, fibre 1g, protein 5g, salt 0.5g

Sticky cherry Bakewell buns

Make our cherry Bakewell buns for a cake sale or to share with friends over a cuppa. These easy, sticky treats are bursting with sweet raspberry jam.

 PREP 30 mins + proving COOK 25 mins   SERVES 12

- 500g pack white bread mix
- 100g golden caster sugar
- 200–250ml warm milk
- 50g salted butter, melted
- 1 medium egg, lightly beaten
- 3 tsp almond essence
- plain flour, for dusting
- a little oil, for proving
- 180g raspberry jam
- 250g icing sugar
- 12 glacé cherries
- 30g flaked almonds, toasted (optional)

1 Combine the bread mix and caster sugar. Mix in 200ml milk, the melted butter, egg and half the almond essence. Add a dash more milk if needed. Knead on a lightly floured work surface for 5–10 mins until smooth and springy. Put in a lightly oiled bowl, cover and leave for 1½–2 hrs until doubled in size.

2 Mix the jam and remaining almond essence. Tip the dough onto a lightly floured surface and squash it down. Divide into 12 pieces, shape each into a ball and roll out to 10cm across. Put 1 tsp of jam into the centre of each and fold in the sides. Pinch the edges tightly together. Put 9 of the buns, pinched-side down, on a lined baking sheet in a circle. Put the last 3 in the centre, spacing them out. Cover and leave for 1 hr until doubled in size.

3 Heat the oven to 200C/180C fan/ gas 6. Bake for 20–25 mins until golden. Cool on the sheet.

4 Mix the icing sugar and 3 tbsp water to make a glossy icing. Spread over the buns, top each with a cherry and sprinkle over the almonds. Leave for 10 mins to set.

Nutrition per serving
energy 318 kcals, fat 5g, saturates 2g, carbs 62g, sugars 40g, fibre 1g, protein 5g, salt 0.6g

Cinnamon rolls

Make our ultimate cinnamon rolls, with toffee edges and plenty of layers. Prepare the day before for warm, sticky buns for breakfast.

 PREP 40 mins + chilling/proving COOK 40 mins   SERVES 12

- 500g strong white bread flour, plus extra for dusting
- 7g sachet fast-action dried yeast
- 1 tsp ground cinnamon
- 50g golden caster sugar
- 1 tsp salt
- 200ml warm milk
- 2 eggs
- 100g butter, softened, plus extra for the tin
- 2 tbsp golden syrup

FOR THE FILLING
- 150g light brown soft sugar
- large pinch sea salt
- 2 tbsp ground cinnamon
- 125g butter, room temperature

FOR THE ICING
- 50g soft cheese
- 50g icing sugar
- ¼ tsp vanilla extract

1 Tip the flour, yeast, cinnamon, sugar and salt into a stand mixer. Mix, then knead until smooth, about 2 mins. Gradually add the soft butter, mixing on medium speed. Flatten to a 20cm square, cover and freeze for 30 mins.

2 Butter and line a 20cm x 30cm tin. Mix the sugar, salt and cinnamon for the filling and set aside 2 tbsp. Beat in the butter. Roll the dough on a floured surface to 35cm x 25cm. Spread over the filling. Fold the bottom edge into the middle, then the top down. Chill for 30 mins.

3 Re-roll the dough to 40cm x 30cm, then roll tightly along the long edge. Cut into 12 slices. Arrange these, spiral side-up, in the tin. Chill for 1–24 hrs. Heat the oven to 200C/180C fan/gas 6. Bake the buns for 20 mins, then scatter over the reserved cinnamon sugar and bake for 10–15 mins until a deep brown colour.

4 Mix the syrup with 2 tsp boiling water. Brush over the hot buns. Beat the soft cheese, icing sugar and vanilla with 1–2 tbsp boiling water to make a pourable icing and drizzle over.

Nutrition per serving
energy 415 kcals, fat 18g, saturates 11g, carbs 55g, sugars 24g, fibre 2g, protein 8g, salt 0.9g

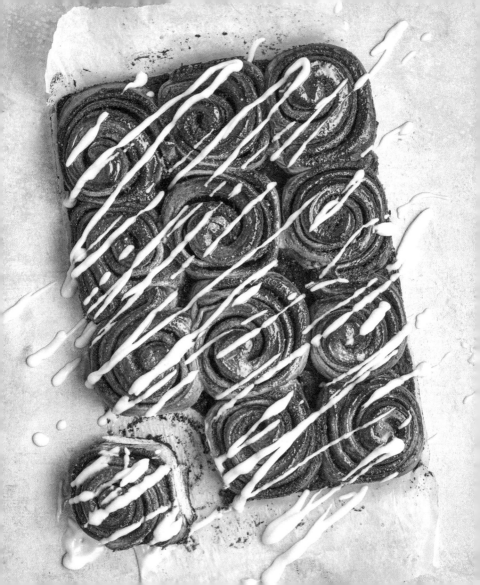

Carrot cake monkey bread

Put a twist on the classic American monkey bread with carrot cake flavours. It's made to be pulled apart and eaten with your hands – like a monkey would!

 PREP 1 hr 20 mins + proving COOK 45 mins   SERVES 12

- 150ml full-fat milk
- 135g unsalted butter, softened, plus extra for the tin
- 550g strong white bread flour, plus extra for dusting
- 1 orange, zested
- 2 tsp mixed spice
- 200g carrots (2 large), grated
- 7g sachet fast-action dried yeast
- 50g golden caster sugar
- 1 tsp salt
- 2 large eggs, room temperature
- oil, for the bowl
- 1 tbsp ground cinnamon
- 100g walnuts, toasted and finely chopped
- 150g light brown soft sugar
- 100g golden marzipan

FOR THE ICING
- ½ orange, zested and juiced
- 100g icing sugar

1 Bring the milk and 85g of butter to a simmer, then cool to room temperature. Mix the flour, zest, mixed spice, carrots, yeast, caster sugar, salt, eggs and milk to a sticky dough. Tip onto a floured work surface and knead for 10 mins until smooth. Put in an oiled bowl, cover and leave for 1 hr, or until doubled in size.

2 Generously butter a 25cm bundt tin. Melt the remaining butter. Mix the cinnamon, walnuts and brown sugar. Divide the dough into 40 to 50 pieces and roll into balls. Roll the marzipan into pea-sized balls. Dunk the dough balls in the melted butter, roll in the walnut mix and drop into the tin, dotting the marzipan balls in between. Cover and leave for 45 mins.

3 Heat the oven to 180C/160C fan/gas 4. Bake for 40–45 mins until risen and golden. Loosen and cool in the tin for 20 mins. Invert onto a plate, leave for 10 mins, then remove the tin.

4 Whisk the orange juice into the icing sugar to make a thick icing. Drizzle over the bread, letting it drip down the sides. Scatter over the orange zest.

Nutrition per serving
energy 477 kcals, fat 18g, saturates 7g, carbs 67g, sugars 32g, fibre 3g, protein 10g, salt 0.5g

Iced buns with cream & jam

Great for a tea party or bake sale. Pipe the cream or use a spoon depending on the finish you want. Best eaten the day they're made, but will keep in the fridge for 24 hrs.

 PREP 45 mins + proving/setting   COOK 30 mins   MAKES 10

- 350ml milk, plus extra for brushing
- 30g butter, cubed
- 500g strong white bread flour
- 10g fast-action dried yeast
- 2 tbsp caster sugar
- ½ tsp salt
- 300g icing sugar
- few drops yellow, pink and purple food colouring (optional)
- 200g lemon curd
- 200g raspberry jam
- 200g blackcurrant jam
- 300ml whipping or double cream, whipped
- glacé cherries, sprinkles or crystallised rose and violet petals, to decorate (optional)

1 Heat the milk and butter until steaming, then cool slightly. Tip the flour and yeast into a stand mixer fitted with a dough hook, then add the caster sugar and salt. Pour in the milk and mix for 5–8 mins on medium speed until the dough is springy. Cover and leave for 1½ hrs until doubled in size.

2 Divide the dough into 10 portions. Roll and shape each into a smooth ball or finger shape. Arrange on a lined baking tray, spaced apart. Cover and leave to rise for 30 mins–1 hr until doubled in size.

3 Heat the oven to 180C/160C fan/ gas 4. Brush the buns with milk and bake for 25–30 mins or until golden. Cool.

4 Mix the icing sugar with 2–3 tbsp water – it should be thick. Divide into bowls and dye each with a different colour. Split the round buns in half or the finger buns down the middle and fill with curd, jam and cream. Spoon some icing over each bun, matching the colours to the jam. Decorate, if you like, then leave to set for about 20 mins.

Nutrition per serving
energy 647 kcals, fat 17g, saturates 10g, carbs 113g, sugars 74g, fibre 2g, protein 9g, salt 0.4g

Chelsea buns

This classic, easy Chelsea bun recipe is the perfect sweet bake to enjoy with your afternoon cup of tea. Who could resist a fruit-filled bun, hot from the oven?

 PREP 25 mins + proving COOK 20 mins   MAKES 9

FOR THE DOUGH

- 450g strong white bread flour, plus extra for dusting
- 2 x 7g sachets fast-action dried yeast
- 50g golden caster sugar
- 1 tsp sea salt
- 150ml warm milk
- 1 egg, beaten
- 50g unsalted butter, melted, plus extra for greasing

FOR THE FILLING

- 25g butter, softened
- 100g currants
- 50g sultanas, roughly chopped
- 2 tsp mixed spice
- 25g caster sugar

FOR THE GLAZE

- 2 tbsp golden or white caster sugar

1 Mix the flour, yeast, sugar and salt. Pour in the warm milk, egg and butter and mix to a soft dough. Tip onto a floured surface and knead until smooth and elastic. Shape into a ball and leave, covered, in a buttered bowl for about 1 hr until doubled in size.

2 Butter a deep 21cm square tin. Tip the dough onto a floured surface, squash down and shape into a 20cm x 30cm rectangle. Spread the softened butter over, then scatter with currants and sultanas. Mix the mixed spice and caster sugar together and sprinkle over.

3 Roll the dough up tightly along the longest edge, then slice into 9 pieces. Arrange in the tin, cut-side up, then cover and leave for 30 mins until doubled in size.

4 Heat the oven to 200C/180C fan/gas 6. Bake for 10 mins, then turn down the oven to 180C/160C fan/gas 4 and cook for 10 mins more until risen and golden. Mix the caster sugar with 1 tbsp water to make a glaze and brush over as soon as they are cooked. Cool in the tin for 10 mins before serving.

Nutrition per serving
energy 363 kcals, fat 8g, saturates 5g, carbs 62g, sugars 25g, fibre 2g, protein 9g, salt 0.62g

Next-level hot cross buns

Forget shop-bought and make your own hot cross buns. The beauty is that you can pack in the spices and dried fruit you want, making them extra special.

 PREP 30 mins + overnight chilling/proving/cooling COOK 30 mins   MAKES 12

- 4 large eggs
- 3 tbsp milk
- 400g strong white bread flour, plus extra for dusting
- 7g sachet fast-action dried yeast
- 50g golden caster sugar
- 1 tsp mixed spice
- 1 tsp ground cardamom
- 1 orange, zested
- 75g raisins
- 75g dried cranberries
- 200g butter, softened, cubed
- 3 tbsp apricot jam

FOR THE CROSSES
- 50g plain flour
- 1 tbsp caster sugar
- small pinch ground cardamom

YOU WILL NEED
- piping bag with a small nozzle

1 The day before baking, whisk the eggs and milk in a jug and put the flour, yeast, sugar, spices, zest, fruit and a pinch of salt in a stand mixer fitted with a dough hook. On medium speed, slowly pour in the egg until it forms a soft dough. Add the butter and gradually increase the speed, kneading for 8–10 mins until the dough comes away from the sides of the bowl and clings to the hook. Scrape off the hook, cover and chill overnight.

2 Tip the dough onto a floured surface. Briefly knead, then roll into a long sausage. Divide into 12, roll into balls and place on a lined baking tray, leaving room between each. Cover with a damp tea towel. Leave in a warm place for 2 hrs until almost doubled in size.

3 Heat the oven to 200C/180C fan/gas 6. Mix the cross ingredients with about 3 tbsp water, adding 1 tbsp at a time until you have a thick paste. Using the piping bag, pipe a line along each row of buns, then repeat in the other direction to create crosses. Bake for 20 mins. Heat the jam and brush over the buns.

Nutrition per bun
energy 368 kcals, fat 16g, saturates 9g, carbs 46g, sugars 17g, fibre 2g, protein 8g, salt 0.2g

Chocolate & spice hot cross buns

Flecked with chocolate, cinnamon, orange zest and plump raisins, these buns make an extra-special Easter treat. Eat on the day you make them or toast the next day.

 PREP 40 mins + proving COOK 25 mins   MAKES 12

- 225ml semi-skimmed milk
- 50g unsalted butter
- 1 large egg
- zest 1 large orange, juice ½
- 450g strong white bread flour, plus extra for dusting
- 2 tsp fast-action dried yeast
- 1 tsp salt
- 50g golden caster sugar, plus 2 tbsp
- oil, for greasing
- 140g raisins
- 100g dark chocolate (at least 70% cocoa solids), chopped
- 1 tsp ground cinnamon
- 100g plain flour

FOR THE GLAZE
- 2 tbsp golden caster sugar
- juice ½ large orange

YOU WILL NEED
- piping bag with a small nozzle

1 Heat the milk and butter until melted, then cool to warm. Beat in the egg and half the orange zest. Mix the flour, yeast, salt and sugar, pour in the milk and stir to a soft dough. Knead on a floured surface for 5–10 mins until smooth and elastic. Leave in an oiled bowl, covered, for 1 hr until doubled in size.

2 Simmer the raisins and orange juice in a pan for 1 min. Whizz the chocolate, cinnamon and 2 tbsp sugar in a food processor until finely chopped. Mix in the rest of the zest.

3 Tip the dough on a floured surface. Press into a large rectangle. Scatter with the chocolate mix and drained raisins. Pull the dough around the filling, then knead until it is evenly spread.

4 Oil and line a large baking sheet. Divide the dough into 12 pieces and shape into buns. Put onto the baking sheet, spaced apart. Cover and leave for 30–45 mins until risen.

5 Heat the oven to 190C/170C fan/gas 5. Mix the flour with 6–7 tbsp water to make a paste, then pipe crosses. Bake for 20–25 mins. Mix the glaze and brush over the hot buns.

Nutrition per bun
energy 332 kcals, fat 8g, saturates 5g, carbs 55g, sugars 22g, fibre 2g, protein 8g, salt 0.5g

Chocolate orange babka

Babka originates from the Jewish communities in Poland and Ukraine and is popular in Israel. It is usually made in a loaf tin, but we've shaped it as a wreath.

 PREP 40 mins + proving/chilling COOK 40 mins   SERVES 14–16

- 550g strong white bread flour, plus extra for dusting
- ½ tsp salt
- 200g caster sugar
- 7g sachet fast-action dried yeast
- 100ml full-fat milk, at hand-hot temperature
- 4 large eggs, room temperature
- 150g unsalted butter, room temperature, cut into cubes
- 3 oranges, juiced
- 1 orange, zest peeled and finely sliced into strips

FOR THE FILLING

- 50g light brown soft sugar
- 30g cocoa powder
- 125g dark chocolate, finely chopped
- 100g unsalted butter, chopped
- 3 oranges, zested

1 Put the flour in the bowl of a stand mixer. Mix the salt into one side of the bowl and half the sugar and the yeast into the other. Turn on low, pour in the milk, then turn to medium and add the eggs, 1 at a time. Mix for 10 mins, then gradually mix in the butter for 5–8 mins to form a soft dough. Cover and leave for 1½–2 hrs until doubled in size, then chill for 1 hr.

2 Melt all the filling ingredients with a pinch of sea salt flakes, then cool and chill for 40 mins, until thickened but spreadable.

3 Roll the dough out on a floured surface to 70cm x 40cm. Spread over the filling and roll up tightly from the shorter end. Cut in half lengthways, open out and cross the 2 pieces over each other like a rope. Curl into a circle, join the ends and transfer to a lined baking sheet. Cover and leave for 1 hr until doubled.

4 Heat the oven to 180C/160C fan/gas 4. Bake for 35–40 mins until golden. Simmer the remaining sugar, the orange juice and zest for 5–10 mins. Brush this syrup over the babka.

Nutrition per serving (16)
energy 393 kcals, fat 19g, saturates 11g, carbs 46g, sugars 19g, fibre 3g, protein 8g, salt 0.1g

Pecan pie rolls

Can't decide between cinnamon rolls and a pecan pie? Why not have both in one bite!
This spiced bake is delicious served warm with a drizzle of icing.

 PREP 20 mins + proving COOK 35 mins   SERVES 10

- 400ml milk
- 1 cinnamon stick
- zest ½ orange, finely grated
- 500g strong white bread flour, plus 4 tbsp and extra
- 50g unsalted butter
- 1 medium egg
- 50g caster sugar, plus extra
- 7g sachet fast-action dried yeast
- 1½ tsp salt
- oil, for kneading
- 5 tbsp icing sugar
- ½ tsp ground cinnamon

FOR THE FILLING
- 5 shortbread finger biscuits
- 100g pecans, chopped
- 100g dark brown sugar
- 3 tbsp maple syrup
- 2 tsp ground cinnamon
- 25g butter, chilled or frozen
- 1 egg, beaten, for glazing

1 Whisk the milk, cinnamon, zest and 4 tbsp flour in a pan and bring to the boil. Take off the heat, add the butter and cool for 10 mins.

2 Pour into a bowl and discard the cinnamon. Beat in the egg, sugar and yeast, followed by the remaining flour and salt. Mix to a soft, very sticky dough. Cover and leave for 10 minutes.

3 Lightly oil a work surface and knead for 5 mins. Put back in the bowl, cover and leave for 1 hr. Heat the oven to 220C/200C fan/gas 7. Line all of a 25cm loose-bottomed cake tin.

4 Bash the biscuits in a bag with a rolling pin until finely crushed. Tip Into a bowl with the pecans, sugar, syrup and cinnamon. Roll the dough to 1cm thick on a floured surface. Grate the butter over and scatter on the pecan mix. Roll up tightly and cut into 2–3cm slices. Lay cut-side up in the tin, cover and leave for 45 minutes. Brush with egg, sprinkle with ½ tbsp sugar and bake for 20–25 mins. Cover with foil and bake for 10 mins. Combine the icing sugar and cinnamon, adding water until it's like thick cream. Drizzle over the cooled rolls.

Nutrition per serving
energy 509 kcals, fat 20g, saturates 7g, carbs 71g, sugars 30g, fibre 3g, protein 10g, salt 0.9g

Belgian buns

Indulge in these moreish Belgian buns as an afternoon treat with a cup of tea. They're filled with lemon curd and topped with icing and a glacé cherry.

 PREP 40 mins + proving COOK 25 mins   MAKES 12

- 450g strong white flour, plus extra for dusting
- 7g sachet fast-action dried yeast
- 75g caster sugar
- 1 tsp sea salt
- 165ml warm milk
- 1 large egg, beaten, plus 1 for glazing
- 50g unsalted butter, melted, plus extra for the tray

FOR THE FILLING
- 5 tbsp lemon curd
- 150g sultanas

FOR THE ICING
- 250g icing sugar
- 12 glacé cherries

1 Mix the flour, yeast, sugar and salt in a bowl. Make a well, pour in the milk, egg and butter and mix to a soft dough. Add a bit of warm water or 1 tbsp flour if it's too dry or sticky.

2 Tip onto a floured work surface. Knead until smooth and elastic. Shape into a ball and put in a lightly floured bowl. Cover and leave in a warm place for 1 hr until doubled in size.

3 Line a large baking tray. Roll out the dough on a floured work surface to 30cm x 45cm. Spread over the lemon curd and sultanas. Roll up lengthways from the shortest side, like a Swiss roll, to form a log. Cut into 12 buns. Egg wash the loose ends and press down, so they doesn't unravel. Arrange, spread apart, on the tray, cover, and leave for 45 mins until doubled.

4 Heat the oven to 200C/180C fan/gas 6. Brush the buns with egg and bake for 10 mins. Reduce the oven to 180C/160C fan/gas 4 and cook for a further 10 mins. Leave to cool.

5 Sieve the icing sugar and mix with 3 tbsp water until thick. Spread over the buns with the back of a spoon and pop cherries in the middle.

Nutrition per serving
energy 363 kcals, fat 6g, saturates 3g, carbs 70g, sugars 39g, fibre 2g, protein 7g, salt 0.5g

Giant cinnamon bun

Take cinnamon whirls to a new level of indulgence with this giant version. Perfect for a party, it takes a little more effort but the results are well worth it.

 PREP 30 mins + proving COOK 1 hr   SERVES 10

- 50g butter, softened, plus extra for the tin
- 200ml milk
- 450g strong white bread flour, plus extra for dusting
- 7g sachet fast-action dried yeast
- 1 tsp ground cinnamon
- 75g golden caster sugar
- 1 egg, beaten
- oil, for greasing

FOR THE FILLING
- 200g light brown soft sugar
- 150g butter, softened
- 2 tbsp ground cinnamon

FOR THE ICING
- 100g icing sugar
- ¼ tsp vanilla extract

1 Melt the butter in the milk, then cool to warm. Tip the flour into a stand mixer bowl with the yeast, cinnamon, sugar and a pinch of salt. Mix in the milk and egg. Knead with a dough hook for 5 mins or until springy. Put in an oiled bowl, cover and leave until doubled in size.

2 Beat the filling ingredients with a small pinch of salt using an electric whisk. Butter a 20cm springform tin. Squash the dough out on a lightly floured surface and knead briefly. Roll out to a 30cm x 50cm rectangle. Spread over the filling and cut the dough into 4 long strips. Roll the first strip up tightly from the short end, roll this in the second strip, and so on, to make 1 large cinnamon bun. Put in the tin, cover and leave for 45 mins–1 hr, or until risen.

3 Heat the oven to 200C/180C fan/gas 6. Bake for 50 mins–1 hr until puffed and golden. Combine the icing sugar, vanilla and 3 tbsp water. Leave the bun to cool in the tin for 10 mins, then remove, drizzle with the icing and cool completely.

Nutrition per serving
energy 486 kcals, fat 18g, saturates 11g, carbs 72g, sugars 38g, fibre 3g, protein 7g, salt 0.4g

Apricot brioche

When toasted and buttered, this delicately flavoured bread is a breakfast in itself.

 PREP 40 mins + overnight proving + 3 hrs COOK 20 mins  MAKES 2 loaves

- 375g strong white bread flour
- 50g caster sugar
- 7g sachet fast-action dried yeast
- 2 tsp salt
- 100ml milk
- 4 eggs
- 175g butter, softened
- oil, for greasing
- 140g dried apricots, diced

1 In a mixer or large bowl, mix together the flour, sugar, yeast and salt, then add the milk and 3 of the eggs and continue mixing to make a smooth dough – 5 mins in the mixer or 8 mins by hand. Add the softened butter and mix for a further 5 mins in a mixer or 10 mins by hand. Put the dough in a lightly oiled bowl and leave in the fridge overnight. Your dough will then be stiff and easy to shape.

2 Grease 2 x 500g bread tins, then divide the dough into about 16 pieces and prod some apricots into each piece. Seal them up and shape into little balls. Place the balls in a tin in sequences of 2 until the tin is full. It should take no more than 8 pieces to fill each tin. Leave the brioche for 3 hrs to prove until doubled in size.

3 Heat the oven to 200C/fan 180C/gas 6. Brush the loaves with 1 beaten egg and bake for 20 mins until golden brown and the loaves sound hollow when tapped underneath. Cool on a wire rack.

Nutrition per serving
energy 216 kcals, fat 11g, saturates 6g, carbs 25g, sugars 3g, fibre 1g, protein 5g, salt 0.8g

Index